CliffsNotes™

Julius Caesar

By Martha Perry and James E. Vickers

IN THIS BOOK

- ■ Learn about the Life and Background of the Playwright
- ■ Preview an Introduction to the Play
- ■ Explore themes, character development, and recurring images in the Critical Commentaries
- ■ Examine in-depth Character Analyses
- ■ Acquire an understanding of the play with Critical Essays
- ■ Reinforce what you learn with CliffsNotes Review
- ■ Find additional information to further your study in the Cliffs-Notes Resource Center and online at www.cliffsnotes.com

WILEY

Wiley Publishing, Inc.

Publisher's Acknowledgments
Editorial

Project Editor: Tere Drenth
Acquisitions Editor: Greg Tubach
Glossary Editors: The editors and staff of Webster's
New World Dictionaries
Editorial Administrator: Michelle Hacker

Production
Indexer: York Production Services, Inc.
Proofreader: York Production Services, Inc.
Wiley Indianapolis Composition Services

CliffsNotes™ *Julius Caesar*

Published by:
Wiley Publishing, Inc.
909 Third Avenue
New York, NY 10022
www.wiley.com

Copyright © 2000 Wiley Publishing, Inc., New York, New York
ISBN: 0-7645-8595-9
Printed in the United States of America
10 9 8 7
1O/RS/QS/QS/IN

Published by Wiley Publishing, Inc., New York, NY
Published simultaneously in Canada

Library of Congress Cataloging-in-Publication Data
Perry, Martha
    CliffsNotes Julius Caesar / by Martha Perry and James E. Vickers.
        p.   cm.
    Includes index.
    ISBN 0-7645-8595-9 (alk. paper)
    1. Shakespeare, William, 1564-1616. Julius Caesar--Examinations-- Study guides. 2. Caesar, Julius--In literature. I. Title: Julius Caesar. II. Vickers, James E. III. Title.

PR2808 .P47 2000
822.3'3--dc21   00--035109
                                                                CIP

Table of Contents

How to How to Use This Book

CliffsNotes *Julius Caesar* supplements the original work, giving you background information about the author, an introduction to the novel, a graphical character map, critical commentaries, expanded glossaries, and a comprehensive index. CliffsNotes Review tests your comprehension of the original text and reinforces learning with questions and answers, practice projects, and more. For further information on William Shakespeare and *Julius Caesar*, check out the CliffsNotes Resource Center.

CliffsNotes provides the following icons to highlight essential elements of particular interest:

Reveals the underlying themes in the work.

Helps you to more easily relate to or discover the depth of a character.

Uncovers elements such as setting, atmosphere, mystery, passion, violence, irony, symbolism, tragedy, foreshadowing, and satire.

Enables you to appreciate the nuances of words and phrases.

Don't Miss Our Web Site

Discover classic literature as well as modern-day treasures by visiting the CliffsNotes Web site at www.cliffsnotes.com. You can obtain a quick download of a CliffsNotes title, purchase a title in print form, browse our catalog, or view online samples.

You'll also find interactive tools that are fun and informative, links to interesting Web sites, tips, articles, and additional resources to help you, not only for literature, but for test prep, finance, careers, computers, and Internet too. See you at www.cliffsnotes.com!

LIFE AND BACKGROUND OF THE PLAYWRIGHT

Personal Background

Many books have assembled facts, reasonable suppositions, traditions, and speculations concerning the life and career of William Shakespeare. Taken as a whole, these materials give a rather comprehensive picture of England's foremost dramatic poet. It is important, however, that persons interested in Shakespeare distinguish between facts and beliefs about his life.

From one point of view, modern scholars are fortunate to know as much as they do about a man of middle-class origin who left a small English country town and embarked on a professional career in sixteenth-century London. From another point of view, they know surprisingly little about the writer who has continued to influence the English language and its drama and poetry for more than three hundred years. Sparse and scattered as these facts of his life are, they are sufficient to prove that a man from Stratford by the name of William Shakespeare wrote the major portion of the thirty-seven plays that scholars ascribe to him.

No one knows the exact date of William Shakespeare's birth. His baptism occurred on Wednesday, April 26, 1564. His father was John Shakespeare, a tanner, glover, dealer in grain, and town official of Stratford; his mother, Mary, was the daughter of Robert Arden, a prosperous gentleman-farmer. The Shakespeares lived on Henley Street.

Under a bond dated November 28, 1582, William Shakespeare and Anne Hathaway entered into a marriage contract. The baptism of their eldest child, Susanna, took place in Stratford in May 1583. One year and nine months later, their twins, Hamnet and Judith, were christened in the same church. The parents named them for the poet's friends Hamnet and Judith Sadler.

Early in 1596, William Shakespeare, in his father's name, applied to the College of Heralds for a coat of arms. Although positive proof is lacking, there is reason to believe that the Heralds granted this request, because in 1599, Shakespeare again made application for the right to quarter his coat of arms with that of his mother. Entitled to her father's coat of arms, Mary had lost this privilege when she married John Shakespeare before he held the official status of "gentleman."

In May 1597, Shakespeare purchased New Place, the outstanding residential property in Stratford at that time. Because John Shakespeare had suffered financial reverses prior to this date, William must have achieved success for himself.

Court records show that in 1601 or 1602, William Shakespeare began rooming in the household of Christopher Mountjoy in London. Subsequent disputes between Mountjoy and his son-in-law, Stephen Belott, over Stephen's wedding settlement led to a series of legal actions, and in 1612, the court scribe recorded Shakespeare's deposition of testimony relating to the case.

In July 1605, William Shakespeare paid four hundred and forty pounds for the lease of a large portion of the tithes on certain real estate in and near Stratford. This was an arrangement whereby Shakespeare purchased half the annual tithes, or taxes, on certain agricultural products from sections of land in and near Stratford. In addition to receiving approximately ten percent income on his investment, he almost doubled his capital. This was possibly the most important and successful investment of his lifetime, and it paid a steady income for many years.

Shakespeare was next mentioned in historical records when John Combe, a resident of Stratford, died on July 12, 1614. To his friend, Combe bequeathed the sum of five pounds. These records and similar ones are important, not because of their economic significance, but because they prove the existence of a William Shakespeare in Stratford and in London during this period.

On March 25, 1616, William Shakespeare revised his last will and testament. He died on April 23 of the same year. His body lies within the chancel and before the altar of the Stratford church. A rather wry inscription is carved upon his tombstone:

Good Friend, for Jesus' sake, forbear
To dig the dust enclosed here;
Blest be the man that spares these stones
And curst be he that moves my bones.

The last direct descendant of William Shakespeare was his granddaughter, Elizabeth Hall, who died in 1670.

Career Highlights

In similar fashion, the evidence establishing William Shakespeare as the foremost playwright of his day is positive and persuasive. Robert Greene's *Groatsworth of Wit*, in which he attacked Shakespeare, a mere actor, for presuming to write plays in competition with Greene and his fellow playwrights, was entered in the Stationers' Register on September 20, 1592. In 1594, Shakespeare acted before Queen Elizabeth, and in 1594 and 1595, his name appeared as one of the shareholders of the Lord Chamberlain's Company. Francis Meres, in his *Palladis Tamia* (a work of criticism published in 1598), called Shakespeare "mellifluous and honey-tongued" and compared his comedies and tragedies with those of Plautus and Seneca in excellence.

Shakespeare's continued association with Burbage's company is equally definite. His name appears as one of the owners of the Globe Theatre in 1599. On May 19, 1603, he and his fellow actors received a patent from James I designating them as the King's Men and making them Grooms of the Chamber. Late in 1608 or early in 1609, Shakespeare and his colleagues purchased the Blackfriars Theatre and began using it as their winter location when weather made production at the Globe inconvenient.

Other specific allusions to Shakespeare, to his acting and his writing, occur in numerous places. Put together, they form irrefutable testimony that William Shakespeare of Stratford and London was the leader among Elizabethan playwrights. One of the most impressive of all proofs of Shakespeare's authorship of his plays is the First Folio of 1623, with the dedicatory verse that appeared in it. John Heminge and Henry Condell, members of Shakespeare's own company, stated that they collected and issued the plays as a memorial to their fellow actor. Many contemporary poets contributed eulogies to Shakespeare; one of the best known of these poems is by Ben Jonson, a fellow actor and, later, a friendly rival.

The question of authorship aside, Shakespeare had an illustrious career in London as both actor and playwright from the 1580s until the 1610s. He began by writing a series of history plays that were meant to chronicle England's past—an ambitious undertaking for a young man. During a forced closure of the theaters in 1592 because of an outbreak of the plague, Shakespeare wrote a long poem, *Venus and Adonis*. This was not his final effort at poetry: Over his career, he wrote a number of long poems, as well as a series of sonnets, which were popular in Elizabethan England. Shakespeare's sonnets were significant for their addressees (a young man and a dark lady), the subject matter, and the complexity of his metaphorical language.

Generally, the early part of Shakespeare's career was taken up, aside from history plays, with writing comedies. One exception, *Romeo and Juliet*, written in 1595 and 1596, is known as a *broken-back* play because its beginning is comic and after the murder of Mercutio, it takes on tragic tones. In addition, Shakespeare wrote a straightforward revenge tragedy, *Titus Andronicus*. Until recently, this play was considered not up to the quality of his later plays, but its reputation has been reclaimed to some degree.

In 1599, *Julius Caesar* was likely the first play to be performed at the newly built Globe Theatre. At the time, England was concerned about questions of unclear succession and consequent civil strife because Queen Elizabeth had neither provided nor named an heir. It is no surprise then, that Shakespeare turned to ancient Rome and their problems with leadership and violence to explore current issues of concern.

During this period, from 1596 to 1604, Shakespeare continued to write comedies, but they gradually began to take on darker tones and, in fact, were not pure comedy but tragi-comedy. The darkness of his writing also took expression in a series of his greatest tragedies such as *Hamlet* (1600–1601), *Othello* (1604), *King Lear* (1605), *Macbeth* (1606), and *Antony and Cleopatra* (1606–1607).

As Shakespeare's career came to an end, he began to write what are now called his *romances*. Harkening back to more traditional romance motifs of quests, magical events, and great lessons learned, these plays are concerned with questions of religion and show a recognition that it is a younger generation who will affect the future.

Shakespeare continued to write until 1613, but his works after the romances are often collaborations, reflecting his retirement from the fray. He'd earned the rest. In a career spanning three decades, William Shakespeare provided works that became the basis of the Western canon of literature and that resonate with meaning for audiences to this day.

INTRODUCTION TO THE PLAY

Introduction

In 1599, when William Shakespeare's Julius Caesar was performed at the new Globe Theatre, Elizabeth I was an aged monarch with no legitimate heir—neither a child of her own nor a named heir. The people of England worried about succession, fully aware of the power struggles that could take place when men vied for the throne of England. They were also aware of the realities of the violence of civil strife.

It is no surprise, then, that the subject matter of this play was relevant to their concerns, even as the content of this play drew on and adapted ancient history. In 44 BC, Rome was at the center of a large and expanding empire. The city was governed by senators but their politics were plagued by in-fighting, and the real glory and strength belonged to generals like Caesar and Antony. In addition, a new group, the Tribunes, had entered the political field. After a hard-won battle, the plebeians, the working class of Rome, had elected these men as their representatives and protectors (as represented by Flavius and Marullus in Act I). The return of the triumphant Caesar and his desire to centralize power went against the grain of the decentralizing that was taking place. Such a setting was fraught with the makings of dramatic conflict.

Shakespeare took this potential for upheaval and used it to examine a leadership theme. Concentrating on the responsibilities of the ruling class, he looked at what could happen if that class no longer had a unified vision and had lost sight of what it meant to be Roman. In fact, the characters of the play lose touch with the tradition, glory, integrity, and stoicism of their past. As you read the play, note the way that Cassius uses the memory of that glorious past to persuade men to become conspirators, and the way that the actions of the conspirators do or do not return Rome to its golden age.

Persuasion, too, is a concept at the center of this play. Everyone seems to be trying to convince someone else of something: Caesar tries to create an image in the public's mind of his crowning (an ancient form of spin doctoring); Cassius finds the best way to manipulate each man he seeks to bring to his side; and Brutus, whom the reader hopes will refuse to participate, takes longer than the others to respond to Cassius' manipulations, but eventually does respond and even finishes the job for him by persuading himself (see his soliloquy in Act II, Scene 1). This pivotal scene, when Brutus joins the conspirators, is also interesting because Portia, Brutus' wife, serves as the voice of Brutus' conscience.

Portia is, in some ways, a stronger character than Brutus and yet, because of her position as a woman in an overwhelmingly male-dominated world, her role is minimal.

If gender is not a central issue to this play, questions of masculinity and effeminacy are. Caesar's weakness—his effeminacy—makes him vulnerable. On the other hand, the incorporation of the so-called feminine traits of compassion and love into the friendship between Brutus and Cassius paradoxically allows the men to show greater strength and allows the audience to have greater sympathy for them. (For a more detailed discussion of this issue see "A World Without Women" in the Critical Essays section of this Note.)

Finally, it is important to have a look at the end of this play and consider what kind of resolution it actually brings. In fact, this approach helps analyze any of Shakespeare's plays. Near the end of *Julius Caesar*, lessons appear to have been learned and Brutus seems to have received his proper due, but audience must not forget that the final speakers, Antony and Octavius, have not always been truthful men and may not be in the future. The ambiguity of the ending of this play is characteristic of Shakespeare's work. The more neatly things seem to be resolved, the more likely it is that the action has just begun.

A Brief Synopsis

The action begins in February 44 BC. Julius Caesar has just reentered Rome in triumph after a victory in Spain over the sons of his old enemy, Pompey the Great. A spontaneous celebration has interrupted and been broken up by Flavius and Marullus, two political enemies of Caesar. It soon becomes apparent from their words that powerful and secret forces are working against Caesar.

Caesar appears, attended by a train of friends and supporters, and is warned by a soothsayer to "beware the ides of March," but he ignores the warning and leaves for the games and races marking the celebration of the feast of Lupercal.

After Caesar's departure, only two men remain behind—Marcus Brutus, a close personal friend of Caesar, and Cassius, a long time political foe of Caesar's. Both men are of aristocratic origin and see the end of their ancient privilege in Caesar's political reforms and conquests. Envious of Caesar's power and prestige, Cassius cleverly probes to discover where Brutus' deepest sympathies lie. As a man of highest personal integrity, Brutus opposes Caesar on principle, despite his friendship with him. Cassius cautiously inquires about Brutus' feelings if a conspiracy were to unseat Caesar; he finds Brutus not altogether against the notion; that is, Brutus shares "some aim" with Cassius but does not wish "to be any further moved." The two men part, promising to meet again for further discussions.

In the next scene, it is revealed that the conspiracy Cassius spoke of in veiled terms is already a reality. He has gathered together a group of disgruntled and discredited aristocrats who are only too willing to assassinate Caesar. Partly to gain the support of the respectable element of Roman society, Cassius persuades Brutus to head the conspiracy, and Brutus agrees to do so. Shortly afterward, plans are made at a secret meeting in Brutus' orchard. The date is set: It will be on the day known as the ides of March, the fifteenth day of the month. Caesar is to be murdered in the Senate chambers by the concealed daggers and swords of the assembled conspirators.

After the meeting is ended, Brutus' wife, Portia, suspecting something and fearing for her husband's safety, questions him. Touched by her love and devotion, Brutus promises to reveal his secret to her later.

The next scene takes place in Caesar's house. The time is the early morning; the date, the fateful ides of March. The preceding night has been a strange one—wild, stormy, and full of strange and unexplainable sights and happenings throughout the city of Rome. Caesar's wife, Calphurnia, terrified by horrible nightmares, persuades Caesar not to go to the Capitol, convinced that her dreams are portents of disaster. By prearrangement, Brutus and the other conspirators arrive to accompany Caesar, hoping to fend off any possible warnings until they have him totally in their power at the Senate. Unaware that he is surrounded by assassins and shrugging off Calphurnia's exhortations, Caesar goes with them.

Despite the conspirators' best efforts, a warning is pressed into Caesar's hand on the very steps of the Capitol, but he refuses to read it. Wasting no further time, the conspirators move into action. Purposely asking Caesar for a favor they know he will refuse, they move closer, as if begging a favor, and then, reaching for their hidden weapons, they kill him before the shocked eyes of the senators and spectators.

Hearing of Caesar's murder, Mark Antony, Caesar's closest friend, begs permission to speak at Caesar's funeral. Brutus grants this permission over the objections of Cassius and delivers his own speech first, confident that his words will convince the populace of the necessity for Caesar's death. After Brutus leaves, Antony begins to speak. The crowd has been swayed by Brutus' words, and it is an unsympathetic crowd that Antony addresses. Using every oratorical device known, however, Antony turns the audience into a howling mob, screaming for the blood of Caesar's murderers. Alarmed by the furor caused by Antony's speech, the conspirators and their supporters are forced to flee from Rome and finally, from Italy. At this point, Antony, together with Caesar's young grandnephew and adopted son, Octavius, and a wealthy banker, Lepidus, gathers an army to pursue and destroy Caesar's killers. These three men, known as *triumvirs*, have formed a group called the *Second Triumvirate* to pursue the common goal of gaining control of the Roman Empire.

Months pass, during which the conspirators and their armies are pursued relentlessly into the far reaches of Asia Minor. When finally they decide to stop at the town of Sardis, Cassius and Brutus quarrel bitterly over finances. Their differences are resolved, however, and plans are made to meet the forces of Antony, Octavius, and Lepidus in one final battle. Against his own better judgment, Cassius allows Brutus to overrule him: Instead of holding to their well-prepared defensive positions, Brutus orders an attack on Antony's camp on the plains of Philippi. Just before the battle, Brutus is visited by the ghost of Caesar. "I shall see thee at Philippi," the spirit warns him, but Brutus' courage is unshaken and he goes on.

The battle rages hotly. At first, the conspirators appear to have the advantage, but in the confusion, Cassius is mistakenly convinced that all is lost, and he kills himself. Leaderless, his forces are quickly defeated, and Brutus finds himself fighting a hopeless battle. Unable to face the prospect of humiliation and shame as a captive (who would be chained to the wheels of Antony's chariot and dragged through the streets of Rome), he too takes his own life.

As the play ends, Antony delivers a eulogy over Brutus' body, calling him "the noblest Roman of them all." Caesar's murder has been avenged, order has been restored, and, most important, the Roman Empire has been preserved.

List of Characters

Flavius and **Marullus** Tribunes who wish to protect the plebeians from Caesar's tyranny; they break up a crowd of commoners waiting to witness Caesar's triumph and are "put to silence" during the feast of Lupercal for removing ornaments from Caesar's statues.

Julius Caesar A successful military leader who wants the crown of Rome. Unfortunately, he is not the man he used to be and is imperious, easily flattered, and overly ambitious. He is assassinated midway through the play; later, his spirit appears to Brutus at Sardis and also at Philippi.

Casca Witness to Caesar's attempts to manipulate the people of Rome into offering him the crown, he reports the failure to Brutus and Cassius. He joins the conspiracy the night before the assassination and is the first conspirator to stab Caesar.

Calphurnia The wife of Julius Caesar; she urges him to stay at home on the day of the assassination because of the unnatural events of the previous night as well her prophetic dream in which Caesar's body is a fountain of blood.

Marcus Antonius (Mark Antony) He appears first as a confidant and a devoted follower of Caesar, and he offers Caesar a crown during the feast of Lupercal. He has a reputation for sensuous living, but he is also militarily accomplished, politically shrewd, and skilled at oration. He is able to dupe Brutus into allowing him to speak at Caesar's funeral and by his funeral oration to excite the crowd to rebellion. He is one of the triumvirs, and he and Octavius defeat Brutus and Cassius at Philippi.

A soothsayer He warns Caesar during the celebration of the feast of Lupercal to "beware the ides of March." He again warns Caesar as he enters the Senate House.

Marcus Brutus A *praetor;* that is, a judicial magistrate of Rome. He is widely admired for his noble nature. He joins the conspiracy because he fears that Caesar will become a tyrant, but his idealism causes him to make several poor judgements and impedes his ability to understand those who are less scrupulous than he. Brutus defeats Octavius' forces in the first battle at Philippi, but loses the second battle and commits suicide rather than be taken prisoner.

Cassius The brother-in-law of Brutus and an acute judge of human nature, Cassius organizes the conspiracy against Caesar and recruits Brutus by passionate argument and by deviously placed, forged letters. He argues that Antony should be assassinated along with Caesar, that Antony should not speak at Caesar's funeral, and that he (Cassius) and Brutus should not fight at Philippi, but he eventually defers to Brutus in each instance. He is defeated by Antony at the first battle of Philippi, and he commits suicide when he mistakenly believes that Brutus has been defeated.

Cicero A senator and a famous orator of Rome. He is calm and philosophical when he meets the excited Casca during the night of portentous tumult proceeding the day of the assassination. The triumvirs have him put to death.

Cinna The conspirator who urges Cassius to bring "noble" Brutus into the conspiracy; he assists by placing some of Cassius' forged letters where Brutus will discover them.

Lucius Brutus' young servant; Brutus treats him with understanding, gentleness, and tolerance.

Decius Brutus The conspirator who persuades Caesar to attend the Senate on the day of the ides of March by fabricating a flattering interpretation of Calphurnia's portentous dream and by telling Caesar that the Senate intends to crown him king.

Metellus Cimber The conspirator who attracts Caesar's attention by requesting that his brother's banishment be repealed, allowing the assassins to surround Caesar and thereby giving Casca the opportunity to stab him from behind.

Trebonius The first of the conspirators to second Brutus' argument that Antony be spared, Trebonius lures Antony out of the Senate House so that the other conspirators can kill Caesar without having to fear Antony's intervention. Consequently, he is the only conspirator who does not actually stab Caesar.

Portia The wife of Brutus and the daughter of Marcus Cato. She argues that those familial relationships make her strong enough to conceal Brutus' secrets, but on the morning of the assassination, she is extremely agitated by the fear that she will reveal what Brutus has told her. She commits suicide when she realizes that her husband's fortunes are doomed.

Caius Ligarius No friend of Caesar's, he is inspired by Brutus' nobility to cast off his illness and join the conspirators in the early morning of the ides of March.

Publius An elderly senator who arrives with the conspirators to escort Caesar to the Capitol. He is stunned as he witnesses the assassination. Brutus sends him out to tell the citizens that no one else will be harmed.

Artemidorus He gives Caesar a letter as the emperor enters the Capitol; in the letter, he lists the conspirators by name and indicates that they intend to kill him, but Caesar does not read it.

Popilius Lena The senator who wishes Cassius well in his "enterprise" as Caesar enters the Senate House. This comment intensifies the dramatic tension in the moments immediately prior to the assassination by causing Cassius and Brutus to briefly fear that they have been betrayed.

Cinna the poet On his way to attend Caesar's funeral, he is caught up in the riot caused by Antony's funeral oration. The mob at first confuses him with Cinna the conspirator, but even after they discover their error, they kill him anyway "for his bad verses."

Octavius Caesar The adopted son and heir of Julius Caesar; he is one of the triumvirs who rule following the death of Caesar. He and Antony lead the army that defeats Cassius and Brutus at Philippi.

M. Aemilius Lepidus He joins Antony and Octavius to form the Second Triumvirate to rule the Roman Empire following the assassination of Caesar. He is weak, and Antony uses him essentially to run errands.

Lucilius The officer who impersonates Brutus at the second battle of Philippi and is captured by Antony's soldiers. Antony admires his loyalty to Brutus and thus he protects him, hoping that Lucilius will choose to serve him as loyally as he did Brutus.

Pindarus At Philippi, he erroneously tells his master, Cassius, that the scout Titinius has been captured by the enemy when the scout has actually been greeted by the victorious forces of Brutus. Thinking that all is lost, Cassius decides to die; he has Pindarus kill him with the same sword that he used to help slay Caesar.

Titinius An officer in the army commanded by Cassius and Brutus, he guards the tent at Sardis during the argument between the two generals, and is a scout at Philippi for Cassius. After Cassius commits suicide when he mistakenly believes Titinius to have been taken prisoner by the enemy, Titinius kills himself in emulation of Cassius.

Messala A soldier serving under Brutus and Cassius, Messala gives information concerning the advance of the triumvirs, and he reports Portia's death to Brutus at Sardis. At Philippi, he hears Cassius confess that he believes in omens. Later, he discovers Cassius' body.

Varro and **Claudius** Servants of Brutus, they spend the night in his tent at Sardis. Neither of them observes the ghost of Caesar that appears to Brutus.

Young Cato The son of Marcus Cato, the brother of Portia, the brother-in-law of Brutus, and a soldier in the army commanded by Brutus and Cassius. He dies during the second battle at Philippi while trying to inspire the army by loudly proclaiming that he is the son of Marcus Cato and that he is still fighting.

Clitus and **Dardanius** Servants of Brutus, they refuse their master's request at Philippi to kill him.

Volumnius A friend of Brutus and a soldier under his command at Philippi. He refuses to hold a sword for Brutus to impale himself on.

Strato The loyal servant who holds Brutus' sword so that he may commit suicide. Later, he becomes a servant to Octavius.

Character Map

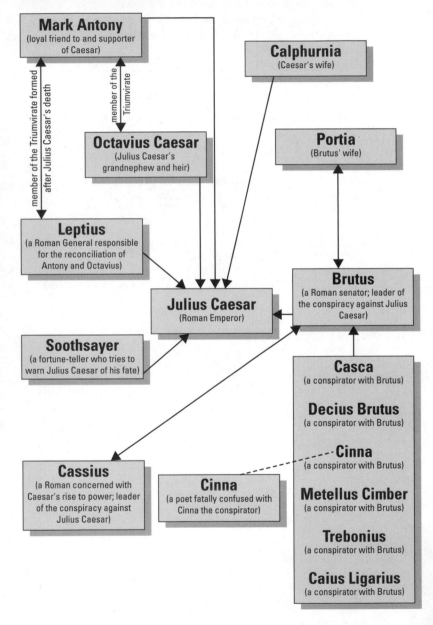

CRITICAL COMMENTARIES

Act I
Scene 1

Summary

On a street in ancient Rome, Flavius and Marullus, two Roman tribunes—judges meant to protect the rights of the people—accost a group of workmen and ask them to name their trades and to explain their absence from work. The first workman answers straight forwardly, but the second workman answers with a spirited string of puns that he is a cobbler and that he and his fellow workmen have gathered to see Caesar and to rejoice in his triumph over Pompey. Marullus accuses the workmen of forgetting that they are desecrating the great Pompey, whose triumphs they once cheered so enthusiastically. He upbraids them for wanting to honor the man who is celebrating a victory in battle over Pompey's sons, and he commands them to return to their homes to ask forgiveness of the gods for their offensive ingratitude. Flavius orders them to assemble all the commoners they can and take them to the banks of the Tiber and fill it with their tears of remorse for the dishonor they have shown Pompey.

Flavius then tells Marullus to assist him in removing the ceremonial decorations that have been placed on public statues in honor of Caesar's triumph. Marullus questions the propriety of doing so on the day during which the feast of Lupercal is being celebrated, but Flavius says that they must remove the ornaments to prevent Caesar from becoming a godlike tyrant.

Commentary

Understand the opening scenes of Shakespeare's plays and you understand what follows: The scene has been painted with brilliant strokes. As *Julius Caesar* opens, Flavius and Marullus, tribunes of Rome, are attempting to reestablish civil order. But it's too little, too late: There is disorder in the streets. The tribunes call upon the commoners to identify themselves in terms of their occupations. In the past, Flavius could recognize a man's status by his dress, but now all the signposts of stability are gone and the world is out of control and dangerous. At first glance, this disorder is attributed to the lower classes who won't wear the signs of their trade and who taunt the tribunes with saucy language full of puns, but while the fickle and dangerous nature of the common Romans is an important theme in later scenes, here the reader is given indications that the real fault lies with the ruling class, which is, after all, responsible for the proper governing of the people.

When Flavius demands, "Is this a holiday?" he is asking whether Caesar's triumph ought to be celebrated. It's a rhetorical question. Flavius thinks poor Romans ought not to celebrate but should "weep [their] tears / Into the channel, till the lowest stream / Do kiss the most exalted shores of all." Caesar, a member of the ruling class, has violently overthrown the government and brought civil strife with him. These issues would have resonated with an audience of the time, able to recall civil disturbances themselves and with a ruler who, by virtue of being a woman, was perceived as less able to rule than a man. (Paradoxically, Elizabeth brought a great deal of peace and stability to England.) In addition, his contemporaries would have recognized that Caesar has overstepped his bounds. Statues of him wearing a crown have been set up before he has been offered the position of ruler, and Flavius and Marullus plan to deface them. Just as Caesar has brought disorder with him, the tribunes contribute to the upheaval by becoming part of the unruly mob themselves.

Why are these statues, erected by supporters of Caesar, set up in the first place? In effect, they are, like modern advertising and political spin doctoring, meant to establish an image of Caesar in the popular imagination. Romans would associate statues with gods and important political figures. Thus Caesar would take on the same associations. In addition, by putting a crown on Caesar before he is actually given the job, the people of Rome are better prepared when it happens. The image already established, Caesar's supporters hope that the event will be more palatable and the transition to power smoother. The act of erecting these statues is part of the process of persuasion and persuasion is a central theme of this play.

Literary
Device

But if persuasion is necessary, it is because political factions are vying for power. This splintering of the ruling class means that there is no longer one common vision of what Rome is and what it is to be a Roman. Marullus draws attention to this problem when he returns to Flavius' original question, "Is this a holiday?" As Marullus points out, it is indeed a holiday, the festival of Lupercal. He is concerned that by disrobing the images "deck'd with ceremonies" he will destroy ceremonies meant not only to celebrate Caesar but also a festival that is part of Rome's history, tradition, and religion. Ceremonies and rituals, in both Roman and Elizabethan terms, were means of maintaining social order, of knowing who you were as a group. By destroying that identity, Marullus seems to sense that he will contribute to the destruction of the state. His intuition is correct and foreshadows the battles to come.

Glossary

(Here and in the following sections, difficult words and phrases are explained.)

mechanical of manual labor or manual laborers.

wherefore for what reason or purpose; why.

triumph in ancient Rome, a procession celebrating the return of a victorious general and his army.

tributaries captive princes who will pay tribute.

Pompey Roman general and one of the triumvirs, along with Caesar and Crassus, defeated by Caesar in 48 BC and later murdered.

sate sat.

vulgar of the great mass of people in general; common; popular.

pitch a term from falconry. A pitch is the highest point of a hawk's flight from which it swoops down on its prey.

Act I
Scene 2

Summary

Caesar, having entered Rome in triumph, calls to his wife, Calphurnia, and orders her to stand where Mark Antony, about to run in the traditional footrace of the Lupercal, can touch her as he passes. Caesar shares the belief that if a childless woman is touched by one of the holy runners, she will lose her sterility.

A soothsayer calls from the crowd warning Caesar to "beware the ides of March," but Caesar pays no attention and departs with his attendants, leaving Brutus and Cassius behind.

Cassius begins to probe Brutus about his feelings toward Caesar and the prospect of Caesar's becoming a dictator in Rome. Brutus has clearly been disturbed about this issue for some time. Cassius reminds Brutus that Caesar is merely a mortal like them, with ordinary human weaknesses, and he says that he would rather die than see such a man become his master. He reminds Brutus of Brutus' noble ancestry and of the expectations of his fellow Romans that he will serve his country as his ancestors did. Brutus is obviously moved, but he is unsure of what to do.

Several times during their conversation, Cassius and Brutus hear shouts and the sounds of trumpets. Caesar re-enters with his attendants and, in passing, he remarks to Mark Antony that he feels suspicious of Cassius, who "has a lean and hungry look; / He thinks too much. Such men are dangerous."

As Caesar exits, Brutus and Cassius stop Casca and converse with him. He tells them that Mark Antony offered the crown to Caesar three times, but that Caesar rejected it each time and then fell down in an epileptic seizure. The three men agree to think further about the matter, and when Casca and Brutus have gone, Cassius in a brief soliloquy indicates his plans to secure Brutus firmly for the conspiracy that he is planning against Caesar.

Commentary

Unrest is possible in Rome because the new leader is weak. The audience is given evidence of this at the opening of Scene 2. Antony is about to run a race (an important and religious element of the Lupercalian festivities) and Caesar calls on him to touch Calphurnia, Caesar's wife, as he passes "for our elders say, / The barren, touched in this holy chase, / Shake off their sterile curse." Calphurnia has not borne Caesar any children, and while in the Elizabethan mind the problem would have resided with the woman, here, Caesar's virility is also in question. The fact that he calls upon another man, known for his athleticism, carousing, and womanizing, suggests that Caesar is impotent.

A lack of virility is not Caesar's only problem. He also is unable to recognize and take heed of good advice. A soothsayer enters the scene and "with a clear tongue shriller than all the music," warns Caesar of the ides of March. Caesar doesn't hear the man clearly, but others do, and it is Shakespeare's ironic hand that has Brutus, who will be Caesar's murderer, repeat the warning. Caesar has every opportunity to heed these words. He hears them again from the soothsayer and even takes the opportunity to look into the speaker's face and examine it for honesty, but he misreads what he sees. The soothsayer is termed a dreamer and is dismissed.

Some critics of this play call Caesar a superstitious man and weak for that reason, but that is not the real root of the problem. All of the characters in this play believe in the supernatural. It is one of the play's themes that they all misinterpret and attempt to turn signs and omens to their own advantage. What characterizes Caesar as weak is susceptibility to flattering interpretations of omens and his inability to distinguish between good advice and bad, good advisors and bad.

Those who surround Caesar are not all supporters. At Caesar's departure, Cassius and Brutus are left onstage. Cassius, whose political purpose is to gather people around him and overthrow Caesar, tests the waters with Brutus. He asks if he intends to watch the race and Brutus is less than enthusiastic. Brutus speaks disapprovingly of Antony's quickness. Cassius, who is a very good reader of other people, interprets this as Brutus' dislike of the new regime and goes on to probe a little further to find out if he will join his group of conspirators. Brutus resists the idea of speaking against Caesar, but Cassius flatters him, suggesting that no matter what Brutus says or does, he could never be anything but a good man.

Their speech is interrupted by a shout offstage and the abruptness of it causes Brutus to display more of his feeling than he may have otherwise. He says that he fears that the people have elected Caesar their king. Cassius has the green light now and presses his case. He speaks of how Caesar oversteps his bounds by calling himself a god when he is only a man and not a very strong one at that. He recounts saving Caesar from drowning. He describes the fever that left Caesar groaning and trembling. Another offstage shout adds urgency to what Cassius says. Brutus is swayed.

Character Insight

With Caesar's return to the stage—not crowned as Cassius and Brutus expect—he looking unhappy and is none too pleased that Cassius is lurking about with "a lean and hungry look." But Cassius is not truly tainted by this description because Caesar goes on to complain that he has not been able to corrupt Cassius and make him fat, luxurious, and distracted by orchestrated spectacles. So Caesar sees Cassius as a good Roman. On the other hand, Caesar worries that "Such men as he be never at heart's ease / Whiles they behold a greater than themselves," and he accuses Cassius of being too ambitious, which makes Cassius not a good Roman. Cassius thus cannot be categorized as good or bad—like all the other actors in this drama, he is complex and very human.

Literary Device

Caesar's insight into Cassius' character reveals Caesar to be an intelligent and effective man, but as Caesar leaves the stage he reveals a physical weakness that represents a moral and intellectual weakness: He is deaf in one ear and can hear only one side of the issue—Antony's. Caesar and Antony exit, with the latter calming Caesar's fears.

The others remain onstage. Casca describes to Cassius and Brutus what all the shouting had been about, how Caesar had to tried to build enthusiasm for his ascent to the throne by pretending disinterest. The plan backfired and the crowd shouted not because they wanted him to be crowned but because they were responding to the theater he had created, as they "did clap him and hiss him, according as he pleas'd and displeas'd them, as they use to do the players in the theatre." The biggest cheer arose when Caesar refused the crown and his fit of pique was represented bodily by a fit of epilepsy.

Casca reveals his own sympathies when he mentions that he had trouble keeping himself from laughing at the scene, and Cassius invites him to dinner in order to convert him to the conspirators' cause.

Brutus, not yet converted, is nonetheless sympathetic and suggests that he and Cassius get together the next day to discuss it further. The scene finishes with Cassius alone on stage. He mistrusts Brutus' nobility and his loyalty to the state, and decides on a ploy to convince him. Having determined the possibility of Brutus' open mind, he will write flattering letters that seem to come from the people and will throw them in Brutus' open window. He could not do this with any hope of success, however, were he not aware that Brutus' mind was open to the suggestion.

Glossary

press to crowd or throng.

ides of March in the ancient Roman calendar, the 15th day of March.

order of the course how the race goes.

passions of some difference conflicting emotions.

conceptions original ideas, designs, plans.

soil to smirch or stain.

by means whereof as a result of

just correct or true.

shadow a mirrored image or reflection.

respect repute.

modestly quietly and humbly, not pretentiously.

jealous on resentfully suspicious of a rival or a rival's influence.

common laughter a frivolous man.

stale make common or meaningless.

protester one who professes friendship.

scandal to disgrace.

rout a disorderly crowd or noisy mob.

indifferently showing no partiality, bias, or preference.

speed me help me forward.

favor appearance or look.

I had as lief I would rather.

accoutred dressed.

hearts of controversy excitement.

Colossus the gigantic statue of Apollo set at the entrance to the harbor of Rhodes and included among the Seven Wonders of the World.

start a spirit raise a spirit.

encompass'd allowed room for.

keep his state maintain a court.

nothing jealous not doubtful.

chidden berated.

ferret eyes red, angry eyes.

marry indeed (an oath based on the name of the Virgin Mary)

gentle noble, chivalrous.

fain with eagerness, gladly.

howted cheered.

chopp'd reddened and chapped.

swounded swooned or fainted.

durst dared.

falling sickness epilepsy.

scarfs sashes worn by soldiers or officials.

quick mettle lively and spirited.

tardy form slow manner.

wit intellectual and perceptive powers.

disgest digest.

several hands different handwriting.

Act I
Scene 3

Summary

That evening, Cicero and Casca meet on a street in Rome. There has been a terrible storm, and Casca describes to Cicero the unnatural phenomena that have occurred: An owl hooted in the marketplace at noon, the sheeted dead rose out of their graves, and so on. Cicero then departs and Cassius enters. He interprets the supernatural happenings as divine warnings that Caesar threatens to destroy the Republic. He urges Casca to work with him in opposing Caesar. When Cinna, another conspirator, joins them, Cassius urges him to throw a message through Brutus' window and to take other steps that will induce Brutus to participate in the plot. The three conspirators, now firmly united in an attempt to unseat Caesar, agree to meet with others of their party—Decius Brutus, Trebonius, and Metellus Cimber—at Pompey's Porch. They are confident that they will soon win Brutus to their cause.

Commentary

Scene 3 opens with the natural world reflecting the unrest of the state. Casca, soon to be a conspirator, is unnerved by what is going on. Cicero, a senator and thus a representative of the status quo, is, on the other hand, blissfully unaware of the danger at hand. It is Casca's task to describe the omens he has seen for Cicero. Cicero's response to that impulse is as follows:

> Indeed, it is a strange-disposed time;
> But men may construe things after their fashion,
> Clean from the purpose of the things themselves.

Style & Language

Cicero suggests that each person will interpret events for their own purposes, and this is, in effect, what happens. Cassius enters the scene and the opening exchange between Casca and Cassius is an interesting one. Cassius asks "Who's there?" and Casca answers "A Roman," identifying himself as a man loyal to the idea of being a Roman—not necessarily one who supports the state as it stands now, but one who embodies all the glories of Rome's past. Cassius recognizes Casca's voice and the latter compliments his ear, reminding the reader, by contrast, of Caesar's deaf ear and his inability to hear, both literally and metaphorically. Thus the reader is left with two contrasting images: Cassius as strong, intuitive, clever; Caesar as weak, deluded, and rather unintelligent.

Character Insight

It is Cassius' cleverness that comes to the fore now. In order to convince Casca of the worth of his cause, Cassius does just as Cicero, the great orator, has suggested men would—he interprets and manipulates the omens for his own purposes. In his hands, all of these frightening events are happening because the heavens "hath infus'd them with these spirits, / To make them instruments of fear and warning / Unto some monstrous state." The monstrous state, Casca is meant to believe, is Caesar's Rome. Cassius tells Casca that there is a man who is "most like this dreadful night, / That thunders, lightens, opens graves, and roars / As doth the lion in the Capitol." Casca asks directly if Cassius means Caesar but, not wanting to reveal himself too quickly and not wanting to leave the possibility open that his words could be turned against him, Cassius allows Casca to draw his own conclusions. Having established the problem, Cassius comes up with a solution. He points out that Caesar is just a man, not a god, and that all of these terrible visions can be overcome by a true, idealized Roman who calls on the spirits of his ancestors for strength and perseverance. Once again, Cassius has found the best way to persuade his listener—in this case, he has called on Casca's image of himself as a noble and loyal Roman, and given him an opportunity to act on it.

Casca joins the plot and the conspirators' faction is enlarged, but to be successful, the person they really need is Brutus. Brutus is well-regarded, wields a great deal of power and, after Caesar is overthrown, has the strength to manage that chaotic and potentially dangerous group, the people. "O, he sits high in all the people's hearts; / And that which would appear offence in us, / His countenance, like richest alchymy, / Will change to virtue and to worthiness." Act I ends in gloom and darkness with the state beginning to splinter. The daylight that Cassius perceives on the horizon is, paradoxically, a light that will show the cracks all the more clearly.

Glossary

sway to rule over or control.

riv'd split.

wonderful that causes wonder.

not sensible not having appreciation or understanding.

glaz'd gazed.

drawn upon a heap huddled.

ghastly ghostlike, pale, or haggard.

howting hooting.

prodigies extraordinary happenings, thought to foretell good or evil fortune.

unbraced with doublet (a man's closefitting jacket with or without sleeves) open.

want lack.

from quality and kind behaving unnaturally.

ordinance an established or prescribed practice or usage.

performed natural.

thews muscles or sinews.

bondman slave, one who is not entirely free of a master.

hinds female red deer.

offal refuse or garbage.

fleering sneering or jeering.

be factious join our faction.

Pompey's Porch the portico of a theater built in 55 B.C. by Pompey.

element the sky.

close concealed.

incorporate a party to.

praetor a magistrate of ancient Rome, next below a consul in rank. Brutus was the chief praetor.

hie to hurry or hasten.

bade bid.

countenance approval, support, or sanction.

alchymy an early form of chemistry, with philosophic and magical associations, studied in the Middle Ages. Its chief aims were to change base metals into gold and to discover the elixir of perpetual youth.

conceited understood.

Act II
Scene 1

Summary

Brutus is in his orchard. It is night and he calls impatiently for his servant, Lucius, and sends him to light a candle in his study. When Lucius has gone, Brutus speaks one of the most important and controversial soliloquies in the play. He says that he has "no personal cause to spurn at" Caesar, except "for the general," meaning that there are general reasons for the public good. Thus far, Caesar has seemingly been as virtuous as any other man, but Brutus fears that after he is "augmented" (crowned), his character will change, for it is in the nature of things that power produces tyranny. He therefore decides to agree to Caesar's assassination: to "think him as a serpent's egg, / Which, hatched, would as his kind, grow mischievous, / And kill him in the shell."

Lucius re-enters and gives Brutus a letter that has been thrown into his window. The various conspirators—Cassius, Casca, Decius, Cinna, Metellus Cimber, and Trebonius—now arrive. Cassius proposes that they all seal their compact with an oath, but Brutus objects on the ground that honorable men acting in a just cause need no such bond. When Cassius raises the question of inviting Cicero into the conspiracy, Brutus persuades the conspirators to exclude Cicero from the conspiracy. Cassius then argues that Mark Antony should be killed along with Caesar; Brutus opposes this too as being too bloody a course, and he urges that they be "sacrificers, but not butchers." It is the spirit of Caesar, he asserts, to which they stand opposed, and "in the spirit of men there is no blood."

When the conspirators have departed, Brutus notices that his servant, Lucius, has fallen asleep. At this moment, Portia, his wife, enters, disturbed and concerned by her husband's strange behavior. She demands to know what is troubling him. She asserts her strength and reminds Brutus that because she is Cato's daughter, her quality of mind raises her above ordinary women; she asks to share his burden with him. Deeply impressed by her speech, Brutus promises to tell her what has been troubling him.

Portia leaves, and Lucius is awakened and ushers in Caius Ligarius, who has been sick, but who now declares that to follow Brutus in his noble endeavor, "I here discard my sickness." They set forth together.

Commentary

While the reader has been led to believe in Brutus' strength of nobility, there is a touch of weakness in the self-delusion he must create before he can join the conspirators: Brutus feels that murder is wrong and so must find a way to justify his actions. It's not for personal reasons that he will do it, but for the general; that is, for the good of the people of Rome. He generalizes about the effects of power and ambition and anticipates the damage that Caesar will do when he gains the crown. He has to admit, however, that Caesar has not yet committed any of these wrongs. Brutus has to convince himself to kill Caesar before he has the opportunity to achieve his ambition; that is, he will "kill him in the shell." The final element of his persuasion comes from an outside source. He responds to the call of the people without knowing that the call is false. The letters that Cassius has penned have been discovered in Brutus' closet; he reads them and is persuaded by them under the same harsh and distorting "exhalations of the air" that light the conspirators' way to Brutus' doorstep. By that light, one can see that Brutus is as tainted as any of the other conspirators.

Character Insight

Brutus, although he has decided to be one of the conspirators, knows that what they plan is wrong. "O Conspiracy, / *Sham'st* thou to show thy *dang'rous* brow by night, / When *evils* are most free?" (emphasis added). But being a man of his word, he is committed to the plan. After a brief, whispered discussion with Cassius, Brutus takes on the leadership of the group, and when Cassius calls on the group to swear to continue as they have planned, Brutus stops them, and begins by a sort of negative persuasion to fix their resolve and establish himself as leader. "No, not an oath!" he says. If their motives are not strong enough, an oath will not help them to accomplish the deed. Only cowards and deceivers would swear, and to swear would be to taint what they do. This is how Brutus convinces his men. He creates a void, takes away what Cassius says, and then fills it with his own voice. By stripping away the words of an oath and by replacing that oath with images of valiant Romans, their very blood carrying strength, nobility, and constancy, Brutus inspires his men and establishes himself as their leader. Caesar, therefore, is not alone in his ambition.

This image of nobility disappears rather abruptly as the conspirators return to the details of the plan. What about Cicero? Should they try to get him on their side? He carries a lot of weight. Perhaps he'd be useful. Maybe they could claim him as the author of what they do and spread some of the responsibility around. Brutus points out that Cicero is too much his own man and will not follow anyone, and so he is excluded. Next, they must decide what to do about Mark Antony. He is a powerful and dangerous foe, but Brutus is doubtful, not wanting to murder for the sake of killing and even regretting that Caesar's blood must be shed.

Literary Device

Blood imagery begins to replace the lightening and flame that dominated the earlier part of the scene. It is as though a bloody rain follows the rumbling warnings of thunder. By means of this fluid image, Shakespeare moves easily between all the connotations that blood offers. The conspirators are up to no good, yet they attempt to lend credibility to what they do by calling on their noble Roman ancestry—their blood—in order to spill Caesar's blood. By this bloodletting, they believe they will regain the masculinity and strength that the state has lost. By penetrating Caesar's body, by exposing his weakness and effeminacy, Romans will be men again.

Character Insight

Just as interesting is the image of blood that Brutus' wife, Portia, brings to the stage. As the conspirators leave their home, Portia sees "some six or seven, who did hide their faces / Even from the darkness." She knows something is very wrong. Brutus hasn't been sleeping well and is drawn from bed "to dare the vile contagion of the night." Her husband attempts to put off her questions but she, among all the characters of the play, seems most able to cut through the darkness and see the truth. "No, my Brutus, / You have some sick offense within your mind." Portia represents strong Roman womanhood, yet can still only be defined in terms of the men around her. She points out that she is the daughter of Cato, a man famed for his integrity, and the wife of Brutus, and for these reasons Brutus should confide in her. Portia's credibility is described in the images of blood. She is Brutus' "true and honorable wife / As dear to [him] as are the ruddy drops / That visit [his] sad heart."

The meaning of this bloodletting is two-fold. First, the audience is meant to remember the Greek myth of the birth of Athena, the goddess associated with both war and wisdom, and who is sometimes described as having been born of the thigh of Zeus. Second, one sees that it is a woman who bears the marks of true Roman nobility. The self-wounding in her thigh is a sort of suicide, an act valued by the Romans as the ultimate sacrifice in the face of dishonor. Portia's honorable bloodletting, then, suggests that the male characters in the play, even though they call on their ancestry and on the ideas of strength and honour, do so in a dishonorable cause. Still, she is a woman, and even though she is "so father'd and so husbanded," she is unable to stem the flow of blood that the conspirators have begun.

Glossary

general the public good.

craves to be in great need of.

crown him that crown him emperor.

disjoins remorse from power separates conscience from authority.

I have not known when his affections sway'd / More than his reason Brutus is suggesting that Caesar is not ruled by passion but is very calculating in his desire for power.

proof experience.

lowliness false humility.

base degrees the rungs upon the ladder he has just climbed. Caesar will turn on the people beneath him.

And since the quarrel / Will bear no color for the thing he is Brutus recognizes that his argument (quarrel) doesn't work (bears no color) because Caesar has not behaved as Brutus suggests he will.

augmented to become greater, increase. Here, when Caesar gets what he wants (is augmented), he will behave as Brutus has previously described.

as his kind according to his nature.

closet a small, private room for reading and meditation, often a study for men, a place of meditation and solitude for women.

exhalations meteors.

whet to make keen, stimulate.

first motion the first proposal of the murder of Caesar by Cassius.

phantasma an hallucination.

The Genius and the mortal instruments / Are then in council; and the state of a man, / Like to a little kingdom, suffers then / The nature of an insurrection Because of Cassius' suggestions, Brutus' mind (Genius) and body (mortal instruments) are in conflict. Thus, he cannot sleep.

brother Cassius had married a sister of Brutus.

moe more.

discover to reveal, disclose, or expose.

For if thou path, they native semblance on, / Not Erebus itself were dim enough / To hide thee from prevention If you show your true nature in your face, not even the darkness of the underworld will be able to hide you from being recognized and stopped.

watchful cares worries that keep them up at night.

fret interlace.

Here, as I point my sword . . . Stands, as the Capitol, directly here Casca's point here is that the sword he points toward the Capitol will, by the violence it inflicts on Caesar, bring about a new day for Rome.

high-sighted haughty, arrogant.

by lottery as Caesar's eye falls on each man by chance.

palter to talk or act insincerely.

honesty personal honor.

cautelous deceitful.

carrions men near death.

insuppressive irrepressible.

or . . . or either . . . or.

several individual.

break with tell our secret to him.

improve make the most of them.

annoy to harm by repeated attacks.

their servants our passions.

ingrafted established firmly.

Quite from the main opinion he held once in contrast to the way he once thought.

That unicorns may be betray'd with trees The story was that a hunter, standing in front of a tree, could lure a unicorn into running at him and then step aside at the last minute. The unicorn's horn would be stuck in the tree.

bears with glasses bears were thought to be vain and would stop to look at themselves in a mirror.

toils nets for trapping.

bent direction.

uttermost at the latest.

rated berated.

by him to his house.

put on our purposes reveal our purposes.

figures dreams.

it is not thus for your health it's not good for you.

with your arms across arms folded, taken as a sign of melancholy.

wafter waving.

physical healthy.

suck up the humors breathe the air.

rheumy dank.

unpurged air that has not been cleansed by the sun.

sick offense an illness, but also a suggestion that Portia knows Brutus is planning to do something wrong.

incorporate and make us one the vows of marriage.

unfold to me reveal, disclose, display, or explain.

excepted unless.

in sort or limitation in a limited way.

suburbs literally outside the walls of the city. The suburbs were often where brothels were situated. Note that Portia refers to herself as a harlot in the second line following.

Cato Cato of Utica, known for his integrity.

counsels secret intentions or resolutions.

constancy steadiness of affections or loyalties.

charactery of my sad brows the sadness that is written on his face.

vouchsafe to be gracious enough or condescend to give or grant.

wear a kerchief to be ill.

exorcist one who summons spirits.

mortified to destroy the vitality or vigor of.

set on your foot take the first step.

Act II
Scene 2

Summary

The scene is set in Caesar's house during a night of thunder and lightning, and Caesar is commenting on the tumultuous weather and upon Calphurnia's having dreamed of his being murdered. He sends a servant to instruct his *augurers*, men designated to interpret signs and appease the gods, to perform a sacrifice. Calphurnia enters and implores Caesar not to leave home for the day. She describes the unnatural phenomena that have brought her to believe in the validity of omens. Caesar replies that no one can alter the plans of the gods and that he will go out. When Calphurnia says that the heavens proclaim the deaths of princes, not beggars, Caesar contends that the fear of death is senseless because men cannot avoid its inevitability.

The servant returns with information that the priests suggest Caesar stay at home today because they could not find a heart in the sacrificed beast. Caesar rejects their interpretation, but Calphurnia does finally persuade him to stay at home and have Antony tell the senators that he is sick. Decius then enters, and Caesar decides to send the message by him; Decius asks what reason he is to give to the senators for Caesar's failure to attend today's session, and Caesar says to tell them simply that he "will not come. / That is enough to satisfy the Senate." Privately, however, he admits to Decius that it is because of Calphurnia's dream in which many "smiling Romans" dipped their hands in blood flowing from a statue of him. Decius, resorting to the flattery to which he knows Caesar is susceptible, reinterprets the dream and says that Calphurnia's dream is symbolic of Caesar's blood reviving Rome; the smiling Romans are seeking distinctive vitality from the great Caesar. When Decius suggests that the senate will ridicule Caesar for being governed by his wife's dreams, Caesar expresses shame for having been swayed by Calphurnia's foolish fears. He declares that he will go to the Capitol.

Publius and the remaining conspirators—all except Cassius—enter, and Brutus reminds Caesar that it is after eight o'clock. Caesar heartily welcomes Antony, commenting on his habit of partying late into the night. Caesar then prepares to leave and requests that Trebonius "be near me" today to conduct some business. Trebonius consents, and in an aside states that he will be closer than Caesar's "best friends" would like for him to be. In another aside, Brutus grieves when he realizes that all of Caesar's apparent friends are not true friends.

Commentary

If Portia is noble, Calphurnia, Caesar's wife, suffers greatly in comparison. She is not so well-husbanded, for here Caesar shows himself to be weak and superstitious. Still, there is truth in Calphurnia's dreams and real caring for her husband in her attempts to keep him from going to the Capitol. Her fault lies in her shrewish nature, which her husband allows to get out of control. Her ability to convince him to stay at home serves to show his weakness.

Caesar shows some vestiges of masculinity, however. Calphurnia describes "fierce, fiery warriors . . . which drizzled blood upon the Capitol," but Caesar responds that "cowards die many times before their deaths." He is determined not be a coward. But as Calphurnia kneels before him, he is persuaded. Here, the reader is meant to remember Portia's actions in the previous scene. She, too, knelt before her husband and he was persuaded. Shakespeare invites the readers to draw comparisons between the two and see a strong woman married to a strong man and a weak woman married to a weak man.

Decius enters the scene as Caesar agrees to feign illness and stay at home. Decius uses all of his powers of persuasion to ensure that Caesar will go out that day. Caesar orders Decius to say he will not come—Caesar seems unable to give one command and follow it through, but is constantly changing his mind—but Decius will not do so unless he can give a good reason for Caesar's non-appearance. Caesar tells of Calphurnia's dream, that "she saw my statue, / Which, like a fountain with an hundred spouts, / Did run pure blood; and many lusty Romans / Came smiling and did bathe their hands in it." Decius reinterprets the dream for him and convinces him that it is a good omen, appealing to Caesar's vanity. Yet even in Decius' flattering description, Caesar is effeminized, for the blood that pours from his statue signifies that "great Rome shall suck / Reviving blood." Caesar is placed in the position of mother, rather than father, of Rome. Convinced, Caesar prepares to go to the Capitol and the tension begins to build. Suddenly, he is surrounded by the men who plan to kill him and his only protector, Antony, enters, tired from the previous night's revels. Caesar, through vanity and weakness, blithely begins the procession to his own death.

Glossary

nor heaven nor earth neither heaven nor earth.

murther murder.

present sacrifice immediate sacrifice.

stood on ceremonies listened to omens.

whelped given birth.

yawn'd opened up.

beyond all use beyond normal experience.

purpos'd preordained.

confidence overconfidence.

happy time at an opportune moment.

stays pauses, tarries, waits, or delays.

to-night last night.

proceeding political well-being.

and reason to my love is liable Decius claims that it is out of love that he tells Caesar this even though he risks anger.

ague a fever marked by regularly recurring chills.

erns grieves.

Act II
Scene 3

Summary

Artemidorus enters a street near the Capitol reading from a paper that warns Caesar of danger and that names each of the conspirators. He intends to give the letter to Caesar and he reasons that Caesar may survive if the fates do not ally themselves with the conspirators.

Commentary

This short scene is tinged with irony. Artemidorus, a teacher of rhetoric, capable of grand and complex flourishes of speech, speaks most clearly and directly. His note to Caesar contains only facts, but has one great fault: For Caesar to acknowledge the facts, he has to admit that he is not a god, providing bloody sustenance to all of Rome, but a mere mortal. That he could never do.

This scene allows you to see another opinion of Caesar. Artemidorus is a Roman who loves Caesar and sees the conspirators as traitors. From this man's viewpoint, the reader gets a hint of the greatness that was once Caesar.

This scene also highlights the public nature of the conspiracy. Given that Artemidorus knows all about the conspirators and their plans, it is made clear that the latter have not kept quiet. Caesar is among the few who do not know what is about to happen.

Glossary

gives way allows conspiracy to take place.

out of the teeth of emulation beyond the reach of the envious.

Act II
Scene 4

Summary

Portia and Lucius enter the street in front of Brutus' house, where Portia is extremely excited. She suggests that Brutus has told her of his plans (in fact, he has not had an opportunity), and she repeatedly gives Lucius incomplete instructions concerning an errand to the Capitol. She struggles to maintain self-control and reacts violently to imagined noises that she thinks emanate from the Capitol.

A soothsayer enters and says that he is on his way to see Caesar enter the Senate House. Portia inquires if he knows of any plans to harm Caesar, and he answers only that he fears what may happen to Caesar. He then leaves to seek a place from which he can speak to Caesar. Portia sends Lucius to give her greetings to Brutus and to tell him that she is in good spirits, and then to report back immediately to her.

Commentary

Character Insight

In this scene, Portia wishes to act but cannot for she has "a man's mind, but a woman's might." Portia's untenable position—her fear that her husband's plan will be discovered (although she does not know exactly what the plan is) and that she cannot act to help him—add to tension at the end of Act II. Caesar is on his way to the Capitol surrounded by murderers. Artemidorous may offer him a way out if he can only hear it and the soothsayer of this scene looks as though he may offer Caesar another chance. What will happen, however, is, so far, only "a bustling rumor, like a fray, / And the wind brings it from the Capitol."

Glossary

counsel a secret.

will crowd a feeble man almost to death there is some ambiguity whether the soothsayer refers to himself or to Caesar.

more void less crowded.

speed thee give you success.

merry full of fun and laughter.

Act III
Scene 1

Summary

Outside the Capitol, Caesar appears with Antony, Lepidus, and all of the conspirators. He sees the soothsayer and reminds the man that "The ides of March are come." The soothsayer answers, "Aye, Caesar, but not gone." Artemidorus calls to Caesar, urging him to read the paper containing his warning, but Caesar refuses to read it. Caesar then enters the Capitol, and Popilius Lena whispers to Cassius, "I wish your enterprise to-day may thrive." The rest enter the Capitol, and Trebonius deliberately and discretely takes Antony offstage so that he (Antony) will not interfere with the assassination. At this point, Metellus Cimber pleads with Caesar that his brother's banishment be repealed; Caesar refuses and Brutus, Casca, and the others join in the plea. Their pleadings rise in intensity and suddenly, from behind, Casca stabs Caesar. As the others also stab Caesar, he falls and dies, saying "Et tu, Bruté?"

While the conspirators attempt to quiet the onlookers, Trebonius enters with the news that Mark Antony has fled home. Then the conspirators all stoop, bathe their hands in Caesar's blood, and brandish their weapons aloft, preparing to walk "waving our red weapons o'er our heads" out into the marketplace, crying "Peace, freedom, and liberty!"

A servant enters bearing Mark Antony's request that he be permitted to come to them and "be resolved / How Caesar hath deserved to lie in death." Brutus grants the plea and Antony enters. Antony gives a farewell address to the dead body of Caesar; then he pretends a reconciliation with the conspirators, shakes the hand of each of them, and requests permission to make a speech at Caesar's funeral. This Brutus grants him, in spite of Cassius' objections.

When the conspirators have departed, Antony begs pardon of Caesar's dead body for his having been "meek and gentle with these butchers." He predicts that "Caesar's spirit, ranging for revenge," will bring civil war and chaos to all of Italy. A servant enters then and says that Octavius Caesar is seven leagues from Rome, but that he is coming.

Antony tells the young man that he is going into the marketplace to "try, / In my oration, how the people take / The cruel issue of these bloody men." He wants the servant to witness his oration to the people so that he can relate to Octavius how they were affected. The two men exit, carrying the body of Caesar.

Commentary

Style &
Language

When the moment of crisis arrives and Caesar enters the public square, the conspirators are pent up and concerned when Popilius wishes them well. Their anxiety is at such a pitch that they are unable to determine what he actually means when he says "I wish your enterprise to-day may thrive." In fact, they almost act precipitously to kill him but are calmed by Brutus who makes them wait to see if Caesar is put on guard. To heighten the crises, Shakespeare shifts from lengthy speeches, asides, and soliloquies to short bursts of dialogue.

The first crisis in this scene is the accumulating danger of discovery arising from the words of the soothsayer, Artemidorus, and Popilius. As that danger is resolved, a graver crisis is suitably expressed in slower and heavier tones. The conspirators ritualistically turn to their prey (Caesar) and mock him with their courtesies. Metellus Cimber kneels before Caesar to press his case that his banished brother be allowed to return to Rome, but Caesar preempts him, mocks him and humiliates him. Cimber is a "base spaniel fawning." There is no suit, really. Instead, Metellus Cimber's actions are a trick on the part of the conspirators to get close enough to Caesar to kill him, and to keep others who may help away. One by one, slowly and methodically, the conspirators come to Caesar, circle him, and kneel. Their words bear all the malice that "sweet words" can afford, during which Caesar shows himself as a self-involved, self-important tyrant.

They kill him, but the murder is not the last crisis of the scene. There is a slight pause in the action for purposes of regrouping, both for the characters and for the audience. The conspirators turn away from the body of Caesar and shout to the populace of what they have gained—freedom and the death of ambition. Before long, however, the specter of danger reappears. Cassius asks "Where is Antony?" Instead of bringing freedom to Rome, the conspirators have actually caused more instability. This group will not hold the state together, and Mark Antony is the troublemaker.

Character Insight

Antony sends a servant to test the waters—better the servant should be run through than his master—revealing Antony as a consummate survivor. This is not to say that he does not truly grieve Caesar's death. His feelings are clear when he views the corpse and sees the murderers, their arms bathed in Caesar's blood. Yet, he is able to cover his feelings, not only so that he can place himself in a position to avenge Caesar's death, but also so that he can find his own position of power. In contrast to the conspirators—even the sharpest of them, Cassius—Antony is strong and politically savvy. Gone are the images of him as womanizer and drunkard. He's taken charge at the moment of greatest danger and he does so by manipulating Brutus' naïveté.

Speaking of Antony, Brutus says, "I know that we shall have him well to friend," but he is wrong—Antony has a plan to persuade the populace to his side at the funeral oration and turn them against the conspirators. Further, while the conspirators weren't very good at keeping their plans to themselves, Antony has been successful. He knows that his ally, Octavius, is on the outskirts of Rome. A military strategy is already afoot. What it is, Antony doesn't divulge, but because Antony tries to dissuade Octavius from entering Rome, the reader may wonder whether Antony does this in order to avoid sharing power.

The ultimate crisis in this scene is the danger that Rome is now in. Consider the way that Antony expresses his grief over his friend's death, indicating that Caesar's body is no longer his own but has become a symbol for Rome itself: "O, pardon me, thou bleeding piece of earth," describing Caesar as "the ruins of the noblest man." No longer flesh and blood, he stands for the breeching of Rome. It is Rome as well as Caesar whose wounds "Which like dumb mouths do ope their ruby lips / To beg the voice and utterance of [Antony's] tongue."

Glossary

schedule a paper with writing on it.

give place make way.

makes to walks toward.

we fear prevention that our plans will be thwarted.

presently prefer immediately present.

address'd prepared.

puissant powerful and strong.

couchings low bows.

preordinance and first decree decisions already made.

law of children rules of a child's game that may be changed and have little consequence.

fond to be so foolish as to.

repealing recall.

freedom of permission.

resting quality stability.

sparks stars, with reference also to the comets of Act II, Scene 1.

Olympus in Greek mythology, the home of the gods.

bootless without benefit, useless.

et tu, Bruté? and thou, Brutus?

common pulpits public platforms.

ambition's debt Caesar got what he deserved.

mutiny uproar.

abide take responsibility for.

stand upon think important.

basis pedestal.

along horizontal.

honest held in respect, honorable.

be resolv'd be answered, have explained to him.

thorough passing through.

untrod state new and unknown state of affairs.

presently at once, instantly.

fears mistrusts.

my misgiving still / falls shrewdly to the purpose I'm usually right about these things.

rank overripe and ready to be cut down, that is, killed.

bear me hard hold a grudge against me.

live if I live.

apt ready, prepared.

mean manner.

pitiful full of pity or compassion.

pity pity pity for Rome was more important than pity for Caesar.

in strength of malice we will be as kind to you as we were harmful to Caesar.

strook struck.

conceit judge.

dearer more keenly.

corse a dead body, corpse.

it would become me better it would be better for me to weep than ally myself with your enemies.

hart a male of the European red deer, especially after its fifth year, when the crown antlers are formed; here, with a play on heart.

sign'd in thy spoil marked with signs of your death, that is, with blood.

Lethe the river of forgetfulness, flowing through Hades, whose water produces loss of memory in those who drink of it; here, Caesar's lifeblood.

cold modesty moderation, the least he could say.

prick'd in number of our friends counted as a friend.

full of good regard right, reasonable.

in the order of his funeral at his funeral.

protest proclaim before he does.

true rites rightful ceremonies.

fall happen.

tide of times course of history.

costly precious.

ope open.

beg demand.

cumber encumber.

in use common.

objects sights.

quartered divided into quarters.

custom of fell deeds commonness of evil deeds.

Ate goddess of discord.

let slip unleash.

passion grief.

try to settle (a matter, quarrel, and so on) by a test or contest.

issue deed.

the which the outcome of the test.

discourse discussion.

Act III
Scene 2

Summary

Brutus and Cassius enter the Forum, which is thronged with citizens demanding satisfaction. They divide the crowd—Cassius leading off one portion to hear his argument, and Brutus presenting reasons to those remaining behind at the Forum. Brutus asks the citizens to contain their emotions until he has finished, to bear in mind that he is honorable, and to use their reason in order to judge him. He then sets before them his reasons for the murder of Caesar and points out that documentation exists in the Capitol that support his claims. The citizens are convinced and at the end of his oration, cheer him with emotion. He then directs them to listen to Antony's funeral oration.

Antony indicates that, like Brutus, he will deliver a reasoned oration. He refers to Brutus' accusation that Caesar was ambitious, acknowledges that he speaks with "honorable" Brutus' permission, and proceeds to counter all of Brutus' arguments. The crowd begins to be swayed by his logic and his obvious sorrow over his friend's murder. They are ultimately turned into an unruly mob calling for the blood of the conspirators by mention of Caesar's generosity in leaving money and property to the people of Rome, and by the spectacle of Caesar's bleeding body, which Antony unveils.

The mob leaves to cremate Caesar's body with due reverence, to burn the houses of the assassins, and to wreak general destruction. Antony is content; he muses, "Mischief, thou art afoot, / Take thou what course thou wilt!"

A servant enters and informs Antony that Octavius has arrived and is with Lepidus at Caesar's house. Antony is pleased and decides to visit him immediately to plan to take advantage of the chaos he has created. The servant reports that Brutus and Cassius have fled Rome, and Antony suspects that they have heard of his rousing the people to madness.

Commentary

Brutus is blithely unaware of the danger that he has allowed to enter the scene. He speaks to the people of Rome in order to make them understand what he has done and why, and with relatively straightforward logic, lays out his rationale before the people and makes them believe that he was right. He describes Caesar's great ambition and suggests to the plebeians that under Caesar's rule they would have been enslaved. Again, the audience is given an understanding of the masses as easily swayed—they do not seem able to form their own opinions but take on the coloration of the most persuasive orator. They are necessary to the successful running of the state, yet they are a dangerous bunch that could turn at any moment. Brutus convinces them of his cause by his use of reason. Even his style is reasonable, here presented in evenhanded prose rather than the rhetorical flourish of Antony's poetry.

Character Insight

Antony is a master of the theatrical. What more dramatic effect could there be than Antony entering the forum bearing the body of the slain leader? No matter what Brutus says, and despite the fact that the crowd is emphatically on his side, from this moment, all eyes are turned to Mark Antony and the corpse he bears. In his trusting naïveté, Brutus leaves the stage to his opponent. What follows is Antony's now-famous "Friends, Romans, countrymen, lend me your ears; / I come to bury Caesar, not to praise him" funeral oration. Antony's rhetorical skill is impressive; he instantly disarms any opposition in the crowd by saying "I come to bury Caesar, not to praise him," but quickly follows this with a subtle turn of phrase that suggests Caesar was a good man and that all that was good of him will go to the grave. He has turned his audience's attention from the "evil ambition" of which Brutus spoke.

Style & Language

Look closely at the rhythms that Antony builds into his oration. Think of Dr. Martin Luther King, Jr.'s "I have a dream" speech, and the repeated emphasis in that speech on one phrase. Antony does the same thing with the phrase "For Brutus is an honorable man, / So are they all, all honorable men" or "But Brutus says he was ambitious, / And Brutus is an honorable man." The phrase is repeated four times, in slightly variant forms, allowing Antony not only to counter each of Brutus' arguments, but also question Brutus' honor simply by drawing so much attention to it.

Finally, Antony incites the mob by suggesting that they have something to gain from Caesar's will. By this means, he initiates desire but must then direct it. He begins to create the desire for revenge and each time he does so, he strengthens that desire by reigning it in. Each time he holds them back, he builds their desire until finally they are passionate enough to do what Antony wants, seek out and kill the conspirators, and, consequently, leave him in power. As a finishing touch, just as Antony created an impressive image by entering the Forum bearing the body of Caesar, he draws his oration to a close by pointing to another image that will remain in the minds of the people as they riot. He reveals Caesar's wounds. As Antony is fully aware, that image speaks far better for his cause than any words possibly could.

Glossary

be satisfied to answer adequately or convincingly.

part the numbers split up the crowd.

lovers friends.

rude barbarous or ignorant.

the question of his death is enroll'd in the Capitol justification for his death is recorded.

extenuated diminished.

enforc'd emphasized.

better parts qualities.

do grace pay respect.

grace his speech listen courteously.

answer'd it paid for it.

general coffers public coffers.

and none so poor to do him reverence No one is so lowly that they owe Caesar respect.

hearse coffin.

Nervii a Belgian tribe defeated by Caesar.

be resolv'd make certain.

dint impression.

gracious drops full of grace, they do you honor.

vesture clothing, garments, apparel.

griefs grievances.

ruffle up arouse.

common pleasures public pleasure grounds.

forms long, wooden benches without backs.

windows historically, shutters.

straight without delay.

upon a wish as I wished.

fortune is merry fortune is kind to me.

are rid to get free from or relieved of.

belike probably.

Act III
Scene 3

Summary

Cinna the poet is on his way to attend Caesar's funeral when he is accosted by a group of riotous citizens who demand to know who he is and where he is going. He tells them that his name is Cinna and his destination is Caesar's funeral. They mistake him, however, for the conspirator Cinna and move to assault him. He pleads that he is Cinna the poet and not Cinna the conspirator, but they reply that they will kill him anyway because of "his bad verses." With Cinna captive, the crowd exits, declaring their intent to burn the houses belonging to Brutus, Cassius, Decius, Casca, and Caius Ligarius.

Commentary

What is surprising about this relatively short scene is its complexity. The purpose of these thirty-eight lines is not simply to show the way in which mob mentality has overtaken Rome—how far ordered society has disintegrated—although violence and intimidation are well represented here in the threateningly rhythmic incantation of the plebeians' questions. The reader can imagine them surrounding Cinna the poet, closing in on him, firing questions from all sides. Cinna's terror is evident in his confused response. This is the realm of mob rule.

Theme

More interesting, however, is why Shakespeare chose to have the plebeians attack an artist. Cinna the poet is being asked to account for himself, not only as a citizen, but as a poet, and he does not pass muster. The plebeians initially attack him as a conspirator, but when they find out who he really is, they are still perfectly prepared to kill him, this time "for his bad verses." Shakespeare has not created a scene of simple mistaken identity. He is asking the reader to examine the position of the poet in this society. To whom must the artist account for his work? What responsibility does he have in making a good and well-ordered society? Who is best able to judge him? These questions were often in the Elizabethan audience's mind. The artist was quite regularly asked to justify himself and his work, and the debate about whether he was dangerous to a stable and moral society was a common one. That the artist would feel the pressure of these demands is metaphorically evident in this scene. Dismembered at the hands of the mob, Cinna the poet is torn as easily as the paper on which those "bad verses" were written.

Glossary

to-night last night.

unluckily charge my fantasy fill my mind with fears.

bear me a bang receive a blow from me.

turn him going send him off.

Act IV
Scene 1

Summary

After they have formed the Second Triumvirate, Antony, Octavius, and Lepidus meet in Rome to decide which Romans shall live and which shall die. Lepidus agrees to the death of his brother, and Antony agrees to the death of a nephew. Antony then sends Lepidus to obtain Caesar's will so that they can reduce some of the bequests. After he exits, Antony tells Octavius that Lepidus may be fit to run errands but that he is not fit to rule one-third of the world; after they are through using him, they will assume the power he temporarily enjoys. Octavius does not want to argue with Antony, but he recognizes Lepidus to be a proven, brave soldier. Antony answers that his horse also has those qualities; therefore, Lepidus will be trained and used. Antony and Octavius then agree that they must make immediate plans to combat the armies being organized by Brutus and Cassius.

Commentary

In his funeral oration, Antony spoke to the people of Caesar's will. He told them of a bequest of money and property to the people of Rome. With blinding speed, Antony seeks to revoke that will, keeping the money and properties for himself, for Octavius, and for the third member of the triumvirate who will rule Rome, Lepidus. In this manner, you can confirm what you may already believe—that Antony has manipulated the people with his own advantage in mind.

The question, then, is not whether these men will respect Caesar's final wishes (they will not), but which of the three men now in power will dominate. Lepidus, who is, in effect, Antony's messenger, sent to retrieve Caesar's will, has no power. The real battle takes place between Octavius and Antony with no clear winner established. So why does Shakespeare concern the reader with this question? Because this power struggle is another aspect of the concern that desire and appetite are at the root of the destruction taking place in Rome. At first glance, one sees only the plebian mob being ruled by passion and standing ready to wreak havoc, but growing evidence shows that the conspirators and the triumvirate are as passionate as the mob.

Despite the fact that Brutus tries to convince himself that he kills Caesar because of logic and reason, he and the others are as much ruled by passion as anyone else. (For evidence of this, see Act II, Scene 1, where their passion is externalized and presented to the audience as disturbances in the natural world.) Brutus is unaware of his own emotional nature and denies it, thus losing its potential power.

On the other hand, Antony is able to accept both sides of his nature and use them to his own advantage. In this scene, his emotional nature can be sidelined when cruel, rational thought is required. How else would he be able to discuss the murders of so many people, the betrayal of so many promises, so easily? Thus Antony embodies both the problem and the solution. He is able to understand and control passion. The Antony who likes drink and women, the Antony who could weep with sincerity over Caesar's corpse, is best able, because of his emotional experience, to take charge.

From Plato through to modern day, reason has been valued over emotional response. Questioning and debating that belief was central to the audience's imagination in Shakespeare's time. Shakespeare is telling his audience that it is possible to live a successful life by combining the two, but also questions what that success entails. The triumvirs, particularly Antony, are more "successful" than are the conspirators, as the audience sees in the next scene; however, this success comes at the cost of cruelty, betrayal, and tyranny. Shakespeare is telling his audience that there is a way to combine the two. It seems as though this group has managed it while the conspirators, as the reader sees in the next scene, are losing control of their feelings. Brutus, in particular, is unable to get a handle on fear, even paranoia. On the other hand, the coldness expressed by Antony and ("He [Antony's nephew] shall not live; look, with a spot I damn him") Octavius ("Your brother too must die"), and even by Lepidus' ("I do consent") to his own brother's death, indicates the horror of men who have replaced their affective for effective sides. The debate is a complex one and not yet complete.

Glossary

triumvirate Group of three men—Mark Antony, Octavius, and Marcus Lepidus—who band together in order to rule over the Roman Empire.

prick'd checked on a list.

cut off some charge in legacies determine how not to pay off Caesar's bequests.

unmeritable weak man, not deserving of the same status as Antony and Octavius.

threefold word divided These three men declared themselves a triumvirate and controlled the empire between them.

sland'rous loads Octavius and Antony are going to use Lepidus to do some of the dirty work that will be necessary.

empty unburdened or discharged; here, relieved of his load.

provender provisions, food.

corporal bodily.

taste measure. Here, Lepidus follows rather than leads.

One that feeds . . . begin his fashion Lepidus is not as up-to-date as Antony and Octavius. He follows trends rather than leads.

property tool.

make head go forward, advance. Here, to raise an army.

combin'd augmented.

made brought in.

how covert matters may be best disclos'd to make plans about how to disclose hidden dangers.

surest answered best met.

at the stake fastened to a stake.

bay'd about surrounded as by baying dogs.

Act IV
Scene 2

Summary

Outside of his tent at a camp near Sardis, Brutus greets Titinius and Pindarus, who bring him word that Cassius is approaching. Brutus complains that Cassius has offended him, and he looks forward to hearing Cassius' explanation. Pindarus, Cassius' servant, is certain that the explanation will satisfy Brutus. Lucilius says that Cassius has received him with proper protocol, but he qualifies his statement, adding that Cassius' greeting was not with his accustomed affection. Brutus says that Lucilius has just described a cooling friendship and he suggests that Cassius may fail them when put to the test. Cassius arrives then with most of his army and immediately accuses Brutus of having wronged him. Brutus responds that he would not wrong a friend and suggests that they converse inside his tent so that "both our armies" will not see them quarreling. The two men then order their subordinates to lead off the armies and guard their privacy, and they all exit.

Commentary

Just as powerful men have struggled for supreme power in the previous scene, here you see the struggle of men as they fall out of love. (It is important to remember that when male Shakespearean characters speak of love, they mean friendship.) Note the type of passionate language used to describe how Brutus and Cassius feel. Brutus says, "Thou hast describ'd / A hot friend cooling. Ever note, Lucilius, / When love begins to sicken and decay / It useth an enforced ceremony." In addition, the imagery of sickness and decay in this quote underscores the potential destructiveness of emotion. The question of how to reconcile passion and reason—the mind and the body—are ultimately unresolved.

Literary Device

Note that this scene stands in contrast to the previous scene, especially in the use of horse imagery. In the previous scene, Antony speaks of Lepidus as a horse as a way of indicating the latter's inferior position. Here, Brutus denounces Cassius as a hollow man, who like a horse "hot at hand, / Make[s] gallant show and promise of [his] mettle." Antony's use of the imagery indicates control; Brutus', a loss of control.

Glossary

he greets me well sends a good man to greet me.

hath given me some worthy cause ... be satisfied Brutus is saying that he feels he has been wronged by Cassius and that the latter ought to explain himself.

regard and honor respect and affection; here, both that Cassius has high regard for Brutus and is himself a man of integrity.

familiar instances tokens of intimacy.

conference conversation.

hollow empty or worthless; here, insincere.

hot at hand lively in the beginning.

fall drop.

jades worn-out or worthless horses.

the horse the cavalry.

gently in a gentle manner; here, slowly.

griefs historically, grievances.

give you audience hear you out with the extra connotation of Brutus as leader hearing the grievances of an inferior.

Act IV
Scene 3

Summary

As soon as the two men are within the tent, Cassius accuses Brutus of having wronged him by condemning Lucius Pella for taking bribes from the Sardians, in spite of Cassius' letters in his defense. Brutus replies that Cassius should not have written defending such a cause, and Brutus charges him with having an "itching palm"—that is, Cassius has been selling offices. Brutus reminds Cassius that it was for the sake of justice that they killed Caesar, and he says strongly that he would "rather be a dog and bay the moon" than be a Roman who would sell his honor for money. The quarrel grows in intensity as Cassius threatens Brutus, but Brutus ignores his threats. Brutus reminds Cassius of his failure to send sums of gold that Brutus had requested for his troops. Cassius denies this and laments that his friend no longer loves him; he invites Brutus to kill him. Finally the two men are reconciled and they grasp one another's hands in renewed friendship.

Brutus and Cassius drink together as Titinius and Messala join them. From the conversation that follows, you discover that Octavius and Antony are marching with their armies toward Philippi and that they "put to death an hundred senators," including Cicero. Messala also reports the death of Portia, but Brutus stoically gives no indication that he already knows of her suicide. He proposes that they march toward Philippi to meet the enemy at once. Cassius disagrees, maintaining that it would be better to wait for the enemy to come to them. This strategy would weary the enemy forces while their own men remain fresh. Brutus persists, however, and Cassius at last gives in to him.

When his guests have departed, Brutus tells his servant Lucius to call some of his men to sleep with him in his tent. Varro and Claudius enter and offer to stand watch while Brutus sleeps, but he urges them to lie down and sleep as well. Brutus then asks Lucius to play some music. Lucius sings briefly, then falls asleep. Brutus resumes reading a book he has begun, but he is suddenly interrupted by the entry of Caesar's ghost. Brutus asks the ghost if it is "some god, some angel, or some devil," and it says that it is "thy evil spirit." It has appeared only to say that they will meet again at Philippi. The ghost then disappears, where-upon Brutus calls to Lucius, Varro, and Claudius, all of whom he accuses of crying out in their sleep. They all swear that they have seen and heard nothing.

Commentary

Portia is dead by her own hand. She's swallowed coals, a most painful—and some would say, fitting—way of death. By her suicide she takes on the sins of the men and attempts to expiate them; that is, in the manner of her suicide she, in metaphorical terms, internalizes the painful, rash, hot decisions that have brought the state to civil unrest. But in doing so, she does not contain and remove the difficulties fac-ing Rome. She is ineffective, for this is not a play about what a woman could do, but a play about men and men's affairs.

The news of her death to Brutus is delayed. For the first one hun-dred and forty-six lines of the scene, the reader is unaware that Portia's death is probably the underlying motivation for Brutus' passionate quar-rel with Cassius. What is Shakespeare's purpose in delaying such news? Impact. The sudden realization of what has happened gives Cassius and the audience a sudden insight into Brutus: the action of the scene and its real motivations and the change in Brutus' and Cassius' friendship. Moments of impact such as these offer a pause, a catching of breath that reveals multitudes.

Character Insight

Note that the love that Brutus felt for Portia is transferred to the male, non-sexual sphere in his friendship with Cassius. Loss and betrayal are essential elements of grief, but Brutus, unable to speak these disloyal thoughts against his wife, transfers his feelings to Cas-sius. It is Cassius who has betrayed him. It is Cassius who leaves him.

Having transferred his grief over Portia into a test of his friendship, Brutus feels that he can go on with the military aspects of his life with stoicism, yet while the feminine is left behind (shown by Brutus expelling the poet because his soft and rounded verses), Brutus still seeks and requires comfort. By banishing thoughts of his wife, Brutus is left with his companions of war. He asks his loyal men to stay with him and looks to Lucius for the calming and expressive quality of music.

Theme

They all fall asleep, however, and leave Brutus to face the ghost of Caesar alone. It is not without some irony that, at this point in the play, Shakespeare allows a male character to experience what has so far been a woman's realm—a prophetic dream. Women, the civilizing influences of art and intuition, have been banned from this world of masculine violence and disruption. In their place, is a man who has put himself in an untenable position by trying to live by reason alone, pushing emotion to one side.

The dream foreshadows—and Brutus realizes—that Brutus will die in the battles to come, and that his death will not be the last. The events Brutus initiated with the murder of Caesar will continue to result in more death.

Glossary

noted historically, branded and disgraced.

letters here, written pleas.

slighted off treated with disrespect or indifference.

in such a case on his behalf or in that type of case.

meet suitable and proper.

nice offense trivial offense.

bear his comment be subjected to scrutiny.

itching palm desire for gold.

mart buying and selling.

honors this corruption makes the corruption seem honorable.

mighty space of our large honors our great reputations.

urge press; here, push.

rash choler quick anger or ill humor.

stares historically, glares.

bouge move, flinch.

observe adhere to.

digest swallow instead of vent.

spleen malice, spite, or bad temper.

indirection dishonesty.

rascal counters worthless coins.

alone on Cassius on Cassius alone.

brav'd defied.

check'd reproved.

conn'd learned.

Pluto the god ruling over the lower world, but here, confused with Plutus the god of wealth.

scope room or opportunity for freedom of action or thought.

dishonor shall be humor I'll interpret your insults as the results of your anger.

lamb a loved person; here, meaning Brutus himself, whose anger is now spent.

vildly vilely; badly.

cynic a member of a school of ancient Greek philosophers who held virtue to be the only good and stressed independence from worldly needs and pleasures. The cynics became critical of the rest of society and its material interests.

I'll know his humor, when he knows his time I'll listen to him with an open mind when he approaches me at the appropriate time.

Companion, hence! Get out!

philosophy a particular system of principles for the conduct of life; here Cassius refers to Brutus' stoic beliefs.

accidental evils pain or troubles happening by chance.

swallow'd fire Plutarch says that Portia died by swallowing live coals.

call in question discuss.

bending their expedition marching their troops.

tenure here, import.

die once die at some point.

art here, philosophic theory.

alive here, of present concern.

forc'd affection the people are not really with us.

under your pardon let me finish.

tried here, got as much support from our friends as possible.

our ventures what we have risked so far.

with your will as you wish.

niggard here, put off or cheat.

knave a serving boy or male servant.

o'erwatch'd overworked and worn out from lack of sleep.

watch your pleasure stay awake and do as you bid.

otherwise bethink me change my mind.

leaden mace a heavy medieval war club, often with a spiked, metal head; here, the music puts Lucius to sleep.

how ill this taper burns reflecting the common belief that a candle's light will diminish when a ghost is present.

hair to stare to stand on end.

bid him set on his pow'rs betimes before Tell him to advance his troops early in the morning, before mine.

Act V
Scene 1

Summary

On the plain of Philippi, Octavius and Antony, along with their forces, await Brutus, Cassius, and their armies. A messenger arrives and warns Octavius and Antony that the enemy is approaching. Antony orders Octavius to take the left side of the field, but Octavius insists upon taking the right and Antony taking the left.

Brutus, Cassius, and their followers enter, and the opposing generals meet. The two sides immediately hurl insults at one another: Antony accuses Brutus of hypocrisy in the assassination and he derides the conspirators for the cowardly way that they killed Caesar. Cassius accuses Antony of using deceit in his meeting with the conspirators following the assassination and he reminds Brutus that they would not have to endure Antony's offensive language now had he died alongside Caesar. Octavius suggests that they cease talking and begin fighting and boasts that he will not sheath his sword until he has either revenged Caesar or has been killed by traitors. Brutus denies being a traitor. Cassius calls Octavius a "peevish schoolboy" and Antony a "masker and a reveller." Antony responds that Cassius is "old Cassius still," and Octavius challenges Brutus and Cassius to fight now or whenever they muster the courage. Octavius, Antony, and their armies exit.

Cassius has serious misgivings about the battle, and both he and Brutus worry that they will never see each other again. They part poignantly with Cassius saying, "For ever, and for ever, Brutus! / If we do meet again, we'll smile indeed; / If not, 'tis true this parting was well made.

Commentary

It is fitting that a battle of words should open the final act of the play. The previous four acts have been largely about words, persuasion, the (mis)use and (mis)interpretation of words, and the power of language. It is no surprise, then, that a power struggle opens the scene as (the younger) Octavius refuses to follow (the older) Antony's orders. The real battle of words, however, occurs between the triumvirate and the conspirators. For example,

- "They . . . would have parley."

- "We must out and talk."

- "The generals would have some words."

- "Words before blows."

- "Not that we love words better."

- "Good words are better than bad strokes."

These passages are taken from just eight lines and are only a small sampling.

Style & Language

Why does Shakespeare so purposefully draw the reader's attention to language? He does so because the question of language and its power were important issues in Elizabethan times. During that period, the ultimate, the most authoritative Word was God's. Human use of language, according to the Elizabethan way of thinking, derived from that authority and thus had within it the potential for a tremendous power—one that human beings both desired and feared. The characters and the action of this play express this desire and fear.

In Act V, by having the two opposing groups speak, Shakespeare tells his audience that, in fact, it is too late for language. Language has already had its effect. It has precipitated violence and no amount of desire for reconciliation (on Brutus' part) or accusation and insult meant to intimidate will change anything. War must come.

Still, lest the readers be left with the impression that human use of language is inevitably all bad, the scene finishes with the poignant parting of two friends, Cassius and Brutus, who know that they risk never seeing each other again. Indeed, by the end of the scene, poignancy returns language to its divine source. Brutus' musing on the end of the battle metaphorically evokes, in this classical pre-Christian context, a desire to know the "end" of all things and the purpose of life, and hints at the possibility of a Christian understanding of an end beyond this life. Brutus' words return the audience to the Word, which in Elizabethan consciousness, informed any and all contexts.

Glossary

battles battalions of soldiers.

answering acting in response or retaliation.

I am in their bosoms I know what they mean to do.

wherefore why.

could be content to visit other places would rather be elsewhere.

fearful bravery a display of courage to hide their fear.

softly here, slowly.

exigent calling for immediate action or attention.

the posture of your blows what sort of blows you will deliver.

Hybla bees bees renowned for the sweetness of their honey. Hybla was in Sicily.

show'd your teeth smiled.

might have rul'd had prevailed.

three and thirty wounds a reference to Christ's age at his death. Antony is suggesting that Caesar has been sacrificed by the conspirators.

a masker and a reveller reference to Antony's fondness for revelry that will become an important element of *Antony and Cleopatra*.

stomachs desires or inclinations; here, their desire to fight.

on the hazard at stake.

Epicurus Greek philosopher and founder of the Epicurean school, which held that the goal of man should be a life characterized by serenity of mind and the enjoyment of moderate pleasure; Epicureans did not believe in omens and portents.

presage foreshadowing quality

former ensign foremost banner.

fell here, swooped down.

consorted accompanied or escorted.

ravens, crows, and kites eaters of carrion and thus inferior to the nobility of the eagle.

as as if.

The gods to-day stand friendly May the gods be friendly.

lead on our days to age live a long life.

incertain uncertain.

reason with the worst imagine and consider the worst.

philosophy a particular system of principles for the conduct of life; in Brutus' case, stoicism.

Cato Brutus' father-in-law who fought for Pompey and committed suicide at Utica. Brutus' stoic philosophy disapproved of suicide.

prevent the time of life cut life short.

stay to wait.

in triumph in ancient Rome, a procession celebrating the return of a victorious general and his army.

Act V
Scene 2

Summary

During the early course of the battle of Philippi, Brutus sends Messala with a message, urging Cassius to engage the enemy forces at once. Brutus believes that the forces under Octavius, which are positioned before him, are currently unspirited and vulnerable to attack.

Commentary

Brutus' actions in this scene embody both hope and the rashness born of having nothing more to lose. It is a short scene, and the very quickness of its language is meant to heighten the tension of the battle for the audience. Remember that in an Elizabethan theater, there was no scenery to shift—the action was fast as actors left and came back on stage, sometimes in a matter of seconds. Remember, also, that the battle, for the most part, takes place offstage. The important action of this final act will lie in the fates of the characters, not in their swordplay.

Glossary

bills statements, usually itemized, of charges for goods or services.

cold demeanor detached in one's outward behavior.

Act V
Scene 3

Summary

On another part of the field, Cassius sees his men retreating; Brutus' forces, having driven back those of Octavius, are foraging about the battlefield for spoils, leaving Antony's army free to encircle Cassius' troops. Thus Cassius sends Titinius to ride toward the soldiers that he sees in the distance and determine who they are, and he asks Pindarus to mount the hill and watch Titinius. When Pindarus reports that he saw Titinius alight from his horse among soldiers who were shouting with joy, Cassius mistakenly concludes that Titinius has been taken prisoner by the enemy. He asks Pindarus to keep his oath of obedience and to stab him. Pindarus does so, and Cassius dies, saying, "Caesar, thou art revenged, / Even with the sword that killed thee."

Titinius was not captured at all, but hailed by some of Brutus' troops when he arrived on horseback. He now enters with Messala, hoping to comfort Cassius with the news that Octavius' men have been overthrown by Brutus. They find Cassius' dead body. While Messala goes to report his tragic discovery to Brutus, Titinius kills himself with Cassius' sword.

Brutus comes onstage with Messala, Young Cato, Strato, Volumnius, and Lucilius and finds the bodies of Titinius and Cassius. To both of them, he pays a sad farewell, calling Cassius "the last of all the Romans." The men leave for another encounter with the enemy.

Commentary

Theme

"Alas, thou hast misconstrued every thing." If earlier scenes were about misuse and misinterpretation of language, this is a scene about miscommunication. Cassius dies because Pindarus misreads the battle and Cassius despairs—a despair that began in Scene 1. Cassius grasps at Pindarus' words as justification for what he desires: death. Titinius and Messala believe that Cassius killed himself because he lost faith in the rightness of their cause and in Brutus' abilities. This interpretation of his death will be all the more hurtful to Brutus.

Character Insight

What is interesting to note is the way in which the audience's views of these two characters has changed since the beginning of the play. Cassius was a dark manipulator of language. His motives for killing Caesar were murky—the readers knew there was more to Cassius' intentions than he admitted. He was emotionless, clinical, and detached; not a friend to Brutus, but a suitor of his power and reputation. At the end, Cassius is prepared to show his great love for his friend and, although this love is noble in itself, it diminishes him to some degree. Note that Cassius' melancholy is the "mother" to his death. In contrast to Brutus' virility in the face of his great friend's death, Cassius is less manly.

Brutus, who at the beginning of the play was passive and pursued by Cassius, is now a man of action. In addition, any doubts that the audience may have had about Brutus' nobility are swept aside by the sympathy gained for him through the powerful friendship he has developed with Cassius.

Glossary

ensign an officer who served as flag bearer.

did take it took the standard.

spoil to seize goods by force.

even with a thought quickly.

ever thick Cassius tells us that his eyesight is poor. He is short-sighted. Note the irony of this phrase, because Cassius will short-sightedly commit suicide.

make to him on the spur move rapidly toward him.

light here, alight.

I swore thee I made you promise.

now be a freeman Pindarus was a prisoner of war and Cassius is offering him his freedom if he will do as he asks.

stand not to answer don't try to change my mind.

change here, exchange of advantage.

apt thoughts of men men who are ready to be deceived.

the mother here, refers to Cassius whose melancholy caused him to accept the false report and kill himself.

own proper our own.

look whe'er he have not crown'd dead Cassius! see how he has placed the garland on Cassius.

Thasos island of Greece in the north Aegean; near Phillipi. Plutarch writes that Cassius was buried there.

Act V
Scene 4

Summary

On the battlefield, in the midst of fighting, Brutus enters with Young Cato, Lucilius, and others. He urges them all to stand upright and brave. He exits, and Young Cato shouts his name and his loyalty to Rome, although some texts credit these lines, showing this loyalty to Brutus and Rome, to Lucilius. Young Cato is killed, and Lucilius is captured by Antony's soldiers who think that he is Brutus. He is then left under guard as one of the soldiers runs to bring Antony to the prisoner whom he believes to be Brutus. When Antony arrives and asks for Brutus, Lucilius tells him that Brutus is alive and will never be taken prisoner. Antony sets guard over the loyal Lucilius, and he sends his soldiers to search for Brutus and report to him later at Octavius' tent.

Commentary

The mistakes keep piling up. In this scene, Antony's soldiers mistake Lucilius for Brutus, the former having taken on the latter's identity in order to protect him, hoping to convince the soldiers that they have captured Brutus, and thus give up looking for him. Antony enters the scene, however, tells the soldiers of their mistake, and robs Lucilius of a noble death.

Now that he is taken prisoner, and not killed, will Lucilius be as valuable a friend as Antony suggests? Lucilius seems the least likely person to switch allegiances, and by the end of the play there is no clear answer whether he will. Antony believes that soldiers will always choose what is best for themselves without consideration for their principles and loyalty. This belief is an indication of the type of ruler he will be— one who is willing to forget both principles and loyalties. Yet Antony gives a glimpse of the decidedly unromantic realities of war. Loyalty lasts as long as the battle, and when faced with the reality of life among the winners, one ought to change sides. These are Antony's perceptions of reality (and are only partially right, as evidenced in the final scene). In fact, his views indicate, to some degree, that when Antony and the triumvirate rule—for they surely will—they will rule a world devoid of the nobility of men like Brutus and Lucilius.

Glossary

bastard here, one who is so cowardly that he will not keep fighting.

only I yield to die I yield in order to die, not to escape death.

there is so much that thou wilt kill me straight here is what will make you kill me (that he is Brutus).

Act V
Scene 5

Summary

Brutus, Dardanius, Clitus, Strato, and Volumnius enter. They are tired from battle, and Brutus whispers a request first to Clitus and then to Dardanius; he wants one of the men to kill him. They both refuse him. He tells Volumnius that Caesar's ghost appeared to him again; he knows that it is time for him to die. Volumnius disagrees, but Brutus argues that the enemy has them cornered, and he asks Volumnius to hold his sword while he runs onto it. Volumnius refuses, believing it an improper act for a friend to perform. An alarm signals the approach of the enemy, and Clitus warns Brutus to flee. Brutus wishes his comrades farewell, including Strato, who has awakened from a quick nap; he repeats that it is time for him to die. Offstage shouts prompt him to send his soldiers onward, and he and Strato remain alone. Strato agrees to hold Brutus' sword; they shake hands, and Brutus runs onto the sword, killing himself.

Amid alarms signaling the rout of Brutus' army, Octavius, Antony, Messala, Lucilius, and others enter and come upon Strato with Brutus' body. Octavius offers to take into his service all who have followed Brutus, and Antony delivers a brief and now-famous oration over the body of Brutus beginning, "This was the noblest Roman of them all." Antony believes that all the other conspirators attacked Caesar because of personal envy; Brutus alone did it because he believed that it would be for the general good of Rome. Octavius promises an appropriate funeral for Brutus and gives orders to stop the battle. Finally, he calls on his colleagues to join him in celebrating their victory.

Commentary

Theme

At the opening of the scene, Brutus is frightened to state his wishes out loud—perhaps ashamed to state his desire to die out loud because he is denying his lifetime philosophy, stoicism, which precludes suicide. This shame would have been prevalent in an Elizabethan audience, to whom the act of suicide would be abhorrent. Still, by running on his sword (note the difference between his death and that of and Cassius, who has Pindarus run the sword through him), Brutus is heroic. To Shakespeare's audience, he would have been a classical, sympathetic, tragic hero, ready to die rather than be conquered. In addition, with a slight shift in perspective, he could also be a Christian hero, sacrificing his life as a result of his decision to fight for the good of the people. (Audiences in Shakespeare's time expected to be able to get more than one meaning from what they saw in the theater and what they read on the page. It was part of the fun.)

In the final analysis, the narrative of both the Christian and the classical hero belong to Brutus and they belong to him because it is "Brutus' tongue" that defines and tells the story. Even though Antony and Octavius have the last word, their praises are, in fact, epilogue.

Literary Device

One addition: Note in Act V, Scene 5, the precariousness of the ending. Shakespeare's finales almost always leave room for doubt, and this play is no exception. Caesar's reputation as a great ruler may have been reclaimed, Cassius' cynical persuasion of the conspirators may have been converted into a great and noble friendship with Brutus, and Brutus' faults may have been glossed over, but despite all the changes effected in this drama, *Julius Caesar* ends as it began—with an uncertain future.

Glossary

remains what is left; here, what is left of my friends.

show'd the torchlight as a signal.

several different.

beat us to the pit driven us to a pit, as in a pit dug to trap hunted animals, or as in a grave.

good respect a state of being held in honor or esteem.

smatch smack or taste.

Brutus only overcame himself Brutus alone slayed Brutus.

saying Lucilius claimed that Brutus would never allow himself to be captured alive. (See Act V, Scene 4.)

entertain to keep up or maintain.

prefer here, recommend.

latest last.

He, only . . . made one of them Brutus was the only conspirator who did what he did out of nobility and integrity.

gentle noble.

the elements any of the four substances (earth, air, fire, and water) formerly believed to constitute all physical matter.

so mix'd so balanced.

use to act or behave toward, treat.

ordered honorably treated with respect.

field a military area away from the post or headquarters.

part share.

CHARACTER ANALYSES

Caesar

In using Julius Caesar as a central figure, Shakespeare is less interested in portraying a figure of legendary greatness than he is in creating a character who is consistent with the other aspects of his drama. If
Brutus and Cassius were eminently evil men insidiously planning the
cold-blooded murder of an eminently admirable ruler, *Julius Caesar*
would be little more than a melodrama of suspense and revenge. On
the other hand, if Caesar were wholly the bloody tyrant, there would
be little cause for Brutus' hesitation and no justification for Antony's
thirst for revenge. In fact, Shakespeare creates in Caesar a character who
is sometimes reasonable, sometimes superstitious, sometimes compas-
sionate, and sometimes arrogantly aloof. In so doing, he has projected
Caesar as a man whom the nobility have just reasons to fear, yet who is
not a villain.

Flavius concludes his criticism of Caesar in Act I, Scene 1, by
expressing his fear that Caesar desires to "soar above the view of men /
And keep us all in servile fearfulness." His opinion is given credence
when, moments later, Casca and Antony's attitude toward Caesar
demonstrates that they consider him a man whose every wish should
be considered a command by the citizens of Rome. Caesar's opinion of
himself throughout shows that he complies with that attitude. He does
not fear Cassius because he believes himself to be beyond the reach of
mere humans, and he caps his explanation of his incapability of expe-
riencing fear by observing, ". . . for always I am Caesar." However, his
reference to his partial deafness provides an obvious contrast between
the conceptions of the vain man who perceives himself in godlike terms
and the actual, aging man who stands in imminent danger of assassination. His potential for evil is further emphasized by the swiftness with
which he summarily has Flavius and Marullus "put to silence." Finally,
at the very moment preceding his death, Caesar compares himself to
the gods of Olympus in his determination to continue his arbitrary
administration of Roman justice.

Caesar's teeming arrogance and pride more than offset his proven
ability to reason. He expresses a fatalistic acceptance of the inevitability of death when he tells Calphurnia how strange it is to him "that men
should fear; / Seeing that death, a necessary end, / Will come when it
will come." But it is not his belief that the hour of his death has been
predetermined and thus cannot be avoided that causes him to ignore
the portents, his priests, and Calphurnia. Instead, he ignores them

because of Decius' challenge to his sense of pride and to his ambition. Caesar, who is so perceptive in his analysis of Cassius, cannot always look "quite through the deeds" of a calculating deceiver.

From his first appearance, Caesar openly displays a superstitious nature, but also from the beginning he displays a propensity to ignore warnings and signs that should alert a man of his beliefs. He enters the action of the play by advising Calphurnia to seek a cure for her sterility by ritual, and he exits fifteen lines later, dismissing the soothsayer as "a dreamer." He ignores the soothsayer, Calphurnia, the many portents, his priests, and finally Artemidorus because he has ceased to think of himself as a fallible human being, and because he passionately wants to be crowned king. He does not fear Cassius, although he knows him to be a danger to political leaders, because he believes that he and Cassius occupy two separate levels of existence. Cassius is a man; Caesar, a demigod. He even comes to think of himself in terms of abstract qualities, considering himself older and more terrible even than "danger." His sense of superiority to his fellow humans, as well as his overriding ambition to be king, ultimately prevent him from observing and reasoning clearly.

Caesar as a viable character in the play endures beyond his assassination. Brutus wants to "come by Caesar's spirit / And not dismember Caesar." In fact, Brutus and the conspirators succeed in dismembering the corporeal Caesar, but they fail to destroy his spirit. Antony invokes the spirit of Caesar first in his soliloquy in Act III, Scene 1, and he uses it to bring the citizens of Rome to rebellion in Act III, Scene 2. The ghost of Caesar appears to Brutus at Sardis and again at Philippi, signifying that Brutus has failed to reconcile mentally and morally his participation in the murder, as well as signifying that his and Cassius' fortunes are fading. Caesar's spirit ceases to be a force in the play only when Cassius and Brutus commit suicide, each acknowledging that he does so to still the spirit of Caesar.

Antony

Prior to Caesar's assassination, Antony makes four brief appearances in which he speaks a total of five lines. Twice during Lupercal and again at Caesar's house, he makes short statements indicating that he is loyal to Caesar as dictator and as a friend. Caesar's confiding to Antony at Lupercal indicates that he trusts Antony and looks upon him as a friend in return, perhaps even as a protégé. Antony appears at the Capitol at the beginning of Act III, Scene 1, but he does not speak before Trebonius leads him out.

When, during Lupercal, Caesar describes Cassius as a dangerous man, Antony defends him as "a noble Roman and well given." While Antony does not perceive at that time that Cassius is dangerous, and later underestimates the determination of Octavius, as a ruler, he is a perceptive observer who verifies Cassius' assessment of him as being a "shrewd contriver." Following the assassination, Antony quickly grasps that he must deal with Brutus, and he has the shrewdness to take advantage of Brutus' naïveté. When he has his servant say that "Brutus is noble, wise, valiant, and honest," it is clear that Antony intends to flatter Brutus and to work upon those personal qualities of Brutus that represent moral strengths, but that are also fundamental weaknesses when dealing with a more sophisticated man.

Antony's requests for safety and for an explanation for the murder are reasonable in the context of the situation, but Brutus' consent to provide both ensures that, upon returning to the Capitol, Antony can concentrate on his ultimate objective of gaining a forum. At the Capitol, by having Brutus repeat his promises, Antony succeeds in placing him on the defensive and in establishing a means to evade the more difficult questions being raised by Cassius. He is not in the slightest degree deterred by considerations of honesty when dealing with those whom he wishes to deceive or manipulate. He knows that Brutus wants to believe that he (Antony) will join the conspirators' cause, and he takes advantage of Brutus' hope when he falsely tells the conspirators, "Friends am I with you all, and love you all." He will also freely use half-truths and outright falsehoods to sway the mob at the Forum to do what he wants.

Antony faces danger in this meeting from Cassius, who knows him to be a "shrewd contriver," and from the other conspirators, who know him to be a friend of Caesar. He disposes of the threat of Cassius by directing his attention to the more powerful and gullible Brutus, whom he keeps on the defensive by repeating that he will be friends if he receives a satisfactory explanation. He disposes of the remaining conspirators by boldly raising the subject of his apparent hypocrisy in making friends with his friend's murderers and by then shrewdly diverting his comments to the nobility of Caesar. This is much in the manner that he will turn the citizens to rebellion by professing that he does not want to stir them up. Antony, in reality, wants two things: to avenge Caesar's murder and to rule Rome. In order to do both, he must first undermine public confidence in the republicans, and second, he must drive them from power by creating a chaotic situation that will allow him to seize power in their place. The method he chooses is to gain permission to speak at Caesar's funeral, and that is the sole reason he plays the role he does in the Capitol.

In his soliloquy in the Capitol, Antony reveals that he intends to create civil strife throughout Italy, and in his oration he sets it off to a promising start. He is thoroughly the politically expedient man in his speech. He wants to create rebellion and overthrow the republicans so that he and Octavius can fill the vacuum, and he succeeds to the fullest measure. From his soliloquy in the Capitol until the end of the play, he is constantly ambitious, confident, successful, and exceptionally ruthless. He has no concern for the welfare of the citizens of Rome who will suffer in the civil strife he has instigated, he is willing to have a nephew put to death rather than argue for his life, he seeks to keep as much as he can of Caesar's legacy to the poor of Rome, and he openly acknowledges that he will remove Lepidus from power as soon as Lepidus is no longer of use to him.

He has some personality conflict with Octavius, but he is able to relegate it to the background so that their differences are always secondary to their struggle to defeat Brutus and Cassius. Antony is also particularly adept at locating the most advantageous point of attack in all of his confrontations. In the Capitol, rather than confront all of the conspirators, he concentrates on Brutus' naive sense of honor and nobility. In the Forum, rather than construct a reasoned argument against the assassins, he appeals to the emotion with which he saw the crowd respond to Brutus' speech. At Philippi, when Brutus leaves Cassius' army exposed, Antony attacks immediately. At the conclusion of the play, when Brutus and Cassius are dead and the republicans thoroughly defeated, he publicly praises Brutus in order to set about healing the political wounds of Rome. Ironically, Brutus hoped to remove arbitrary government from Rome by the assassination, but by murdering Caesar, he established the conditions for an even more ruthless tyranny to seize power in the persons of Antony and Octavius.

Octavius

Julius Caesar is its own frame of reference, and a knowledge of Roman history is not essential to an understanding of the play. However, Shakespeare does construct the character of Octavius by highlighting those aspects of his personality that will predominate later in his political and military conflicts with Antony and in his role as the Emperor Augustus. In order to stabilize the political situation in Rome following the assassination and to solidify the triumvirs' control of government, Octavius is willing to conduct a ruthless reign of terror during which the opponents to the triumvirs are methodically slaughtered, but not all of those on the proscription list are actual enemies. Some are simply wealthy Romans who are condemned as "traitors" and executed in order that the triumvirs may confiscate their estates as a means of raising money to finance their armies. It is, nevertheless, noteworthy that the future Augustus does not volunteer members of his own immediate family to the list, although he does insist on the death of Lepidus' brother and does not object to the inclusion of Antony's nephew.

Octavius exhibits creditable insight in his observation that all who currently act friendly to the triumvirs are not indeed friends and in his attitude toward Antony throughout the play. He knows that he is in a power struggle with Antony that will intensify after they have defeated their enemies, and he knows enough about Antony's thirst for power to protect himself from domination by Antony. Consequently, he is not reluctant to disagree with Antony, as he demonstrates in his defense of Lepidus ("he's a tried and valiant soldier"), in his pointing to Antony's error in predicting that Brutus and Cassius would not come to Philippi, and in his insistence that he will fight on the right-hand side of the battlefield at Philippi and not the left-hand side as Antony orders. However, Octavius does not let his determination to remain independent interfere with following Antony's advice when he realizes that Antony speaks from experience, as he demonstrates in agreeing to allow Antony to make Lepidus a junior partner in the Triumvirate, in agreeing with Antony that the most important matter at hand following the assassination is to prepare to meet the republican armies, and in accepting Antony's decision that they should fight from defensive positions at Philippi and allow the enemy to initiate the battle.

Octavius is shrewd in his political assessments and in his relationship with Antony. He is decisive in executing the proscription and in preparing to meet Brutus and Cassius. He is also supremely confident that he will succeed in defeating his enemies at Philippi and in organizing a successful new government of Rome.

Brutus

Brutus is the most complex of the characters in this play. He is proud of his reputation for honor and nobleness, but he is not always practical, and is often naive. He is the only major character in the play intensely committed to fashioning his behavior to fit a strict moral and ethical code, but he take actions that are unconsciously hypocritical. One of the significant themes that Shakespeare uses to enrich the complexity of Brutus involves his attempt to ritualize the assassination of Caesar. He cannot justify, to his own satisfaction, the murder of a man who is a friend and who has not excessively misused the powers of his office. Consequently, thinking of the assassination in terms of a quasi-religious ritual instead of cold-blooded murder makes it more acceptable to him. Unfortunately for him, he consistently misjudges the people and the citizens of Rome; he believes that they will be willing to consider the assassination in abstract terms.

Brutus is guided in all things by his concepts of honor. He speaks of them often to Cassius, and he is greatly disturbed when events force him to act in a manner inconsistent with them. Consider his anguish when he drinks a toast with Caesar while wearing a false face to hide his complicity in the conspiracy. Ironically, his widely reputed honor is what causes Cassius to make an all-out effort to bring him into an enterprise of debatable moral respectability. Brutus' reputation is so great that it will act to convince others who are as yet undecided to join.

Brutus' concentration on honorable and noble behavior also leads him into assuming a naive view of the world. He is unable to see through the roles being played by Cassius, Casca, and Antony. He does not recognize the bogus letters as having been sent by Cassius, although they contain sentiments and diction that would warn a more perceptive man. He underestimates Antony as an opponent, and he loses control over the discussion at the Capitol following the assassination by meeting Antony's requests too readily. Brutus as a naive thinker is most clearly revealed in the scene in the Forum. He presents his reasons for the assassination, and he leaves believing that he has satisfied the Roman citizens with his reasoned oration. He does not realize that his speech has only moved the mob emotionally; it has not prodded them to make reasoned assessments of what the conspirators have done.

Brutus is endowed with qualities that could make him a successful private man but that limit him severely, even fatally, when he endeavors to compete in public life with those who do not choose to act with the same ethical and moral considerations. In his scene with Portia, Brutus shows that he has already become alienated with his once happy home life because of his concentration on his "enterprise," which will eventually cause him to lose everything except the belief that he has acted honorably and nobly. In the tent at Sardis, after learning of Portia's death and believing that Cassius is bringing discredit on the republican cause, Brutus becomes most isolated. His private life is destroyed, and he also has difficulty avoiding the taint of dishonor in his public life.

Brutus makes moral decisions slowly, and he is continually at war with himself even after he has decided on a course of action. He has been thinking about the problem that Caesar represents to Roman liberty for an unspecified time when the play opens. After Cassius raises the subject and asks for Brutus' commitment, he requests time to think the matter over, and a month later, speaking alone in his orchard, he reveals that he has since thought of little else. He has trouble arriving at a decision whether to participate in the assassination, he expresses contradictory attitudes towards the conspiracy, he attempts to "purify" the murder through ritual, and he condemns Cassius' money-raising practices while asking for a share. His final words, "Caesar, now be still: / I kill'd not thee with half so good a will," are almost a supplication for an end to his mental torture.

On the other hand, Brutus characteristically makes decisions that are essential to his and Cassius' success with much less forethought, and after he's committed to a plan, he does not waiver. He quickly takes command of the conspiracy and makes crucial decisions regarding Cicero and Antony. He does not, however, make adequate plans to solidify republican control of government following the assassination, and he too readily agrees to allow Antony to speak.

Brutus' character is made even more complex by his unconscious hypocrisy. He has conflicting attitudes toward the conspiracy, but he becomes more favorable following his becoming a member of the plot against Caesar. He attacks Cassius for raising money dishonestly, yet he demands a portion. Nevertheless, at the end, Brutus is a man who nobly accepts his fate. He dismisses the ghost of Caesar at Sardis. He chooses personal honor over a strict adherence to an abstract philosophy. He reacts calmly and reasonably to Cassius' death, as he had earlier in a moment of crisis when Popilius revealed that the conspiracy was no longer secret. In his last moments, he has the satisfaction of being certain in his own mind that he has been faithful to the principles embodying the honor and nobility on which he has placed so much value throughout his life.

Cassius

The most significant characteristic of Cassius is his ability to perceive the true motives of men. Caesar says of him, "He reads much; / He is a great observer and he looks / Quite through the deeds of men." The great irony surrounding Cassius throughout the play is that he nullifies his greatest asset when he allows Brutus to take effective control of the republican faction.

Cassius believes that the nobility of Rome are responsible for the government of Rome. They have allowed a man to gain excessive power; therefore, they have the responsibility to stop him, and with a man of Caesar's well-known ambition, that can only mean assassination.

Cassius intensely dislikes Caesar personally, but he also deeply resents being subservient to a tyrant, and there are indications that he would fight for his personal freedom under any tyrant. He does not resent following the almost dictatorial pronouncements of his equal, Brutus, although he does disagree heatedly with most of Brutus' tactical decisions. To accomplish his goal of removing Caesar from power, he resorts to using his keen insight into human nature to deceive Brutus by means of a long and passionate argument, coupled with bogus notes. In the conversation, he appeals to Brutus' sense of honor, nobility, and pride more than he presents concrete examples of Caesar's tyrannical actions. Later, he is more outrightly devious in the use of forged notes, the last of which prompts Brutus to leave off contemplation and to join the conspiracy. Cassius later uses similar means to bring Casca into the plot.

Throughout the action, Cassius remains relatively unconcerned with the unscrupulous means he is willing to use to further the republican cause, and at Sardis, he and Brutus come almost to breaking up their alliance because Brutus objects to his ways of collecting revenue to support the armies. Cassius sees Brutus as the catalyst that will unite the leading nobles in a conspiracy, and he makes the recruitment of Brutus his first priority. Ironically, his success leads directly to a continuous decline of his own influence within the republican camp.

Clearly, Cassius has his negative aspects. He envies Caesar; he becomes an assassin; and he will consent to bribery, sell commissions, and impose ruinous taxation to raise money. But he also has a certain nobility of mind that is generally recognized. When Caesar tells Antony that Cassius is dangerous, Antony answers, "Fear him not, Caesar; he's not dangerous. / He's a noble Roman and well given." He was no doubt expressing sentiments popular at the time. Cassius is also highly emotional. He displays extreme hatred in his verbal attack on Caesar during Lupercal; he almost loses control because of fear when Popilius reveals that the conspirators' plans have been leaked; he gives vent to anger in his argument with Brutus in the tent at Sardis; he expresses an understanding tolerance of the poet who pleads for him and Brutus to stop their quarrel; and he threatens suicide repeatedly and finally chooses self-inflicted death to humiliating capture by Antony and Octavius. When he becomes a genuine friend of Brutus following the reconciliation in the tent, he remains faithful and refuses to blame Brutus for the dilemma that he encounters at Philippi, even though he has reason to do so.

Of all the leading characters in Julius Caesar, Cassius develops most as the action progresses. At the end of Act I, Scene 2, he is a passionate and devious manipulator striving to use Brutus to gain his ends. By the end of Act IV, Scene 3, he is a calm friend of Brutus who will remain faithful to their friendship until death.

CRITICAL ESSAYS

Who's In Charge Here?

Who's in charge, who ought to be in charge, and how well are those in charge doing? These are central questions in *Julius Caesar*. The Elizabethan expectation would be that the ruling class ought to rule and that they ought to rule in the best interests of the people. Such is not the case in the Rome of this play. Barely controlled chaos has come to Rome, and this unsettled state is personified in the first scene of *Julius Caesar* through the characters of the cobbler and the carpenter. These characters give readers a sense that the people themselves are a sort of amorphous mass, potentially dangerous and, at the same time, absolutely essential to the success of the ruling class. Throughout the play, they are addressed: Caesar must give them entertainment and seeks their approbation for his crowning, Brutus recognizes that he must explain his actions to them, and Antony uses them for his own purposes. Yet, despite the plebeians' surging power, real chaos actually lies in the failure of the ruling class to exercise their authority properly and to live by the accepted rules of hierarchy and order.

These same threats and concerns resonated to an Elizabethan audience. At the time this play was performed in 1599, civil strife was within living memory. Henry VIII's reformation of the Church of England had brought violence and unrest to the country. In addition, despite all of his efforts, Henry had not provided a living and legitimate male heir for England. At his death, his daughter Mary returned the church to the bosom of Rome, demanding that her subjects align themselves with Catholicism. When Mary, too, died without heir, her sister, Elizabeth, took the throne. What followed was a long period, from 1548 to her death in 1603, of relative peace and prosperity. However, Elizabeth's subjects experienced unease during her reign. She was, after all, a woman, and according to the Elizabethan understanding of order, men ruled women, not the other way around.

Her subjects wished for Elizabeth to marry for a number of reasons. They would have felt much more secure knowing that a man was in charge, but further, they were tired of worries over succession. A legitimate heir was necessary. The Queen, on the other hand, over the period of her fertility refused the suits of a number of appropriate men, knowing that once married, she would no longer rule the realm. By the time this play was performed Elizabeth was an old woman, well beyond the age of childbearing. Even then, she refused to name an heir and the country worried that they would face another period of unrest at her death.

But even without this historical context, Elizabethans would have been interested in questions of order and hierarchy—questions raised by the political upheaval of *Julius Caesar*. The Elizabethan worldview was one in which everyone had their place. In many ways, they understood the world in terms of the family unit. God was the head of the heavenly family, with Jesus as his son. The monarch was subservient only to God, receiving power to head the English family from Him. The monarch's subjects maintained their kingdoms through the various levels of society and finally into their own homes, with men ruling their wives and wives ruling their children. Elizabethan thinking went so far as to order all living things in a hierarchy known as the *Great Chain of Being*, from God and the various levels of angels right through to the lowliest animal. In such a rigidly structured society it is entirely understandable that its members would be interested in exploring and examining the potentials of and the excitement that would be provided by an inversion of that order.

On the other hand, while it would have been acceptable to examine this relatively objective philosophical issue in the public theater, it would have been much less acceptable (to say the least) to set it within the context of the history of their own period. No direct questioning of England's state or monarch would have been possible. Playwrights of the time were aware of the dilemma and crafted their plays so that they would not offend. The setting of this play, therefore, in ancient Rome was the perfect answer. The story, taken from the Roman historian, Plutarch's, work called *Lives*, was well known to Shakespeare's audience, full of drama and conflict, and was sufficiently distant in time to allow both Shakespeare and his audience to operate in safety.

Now, on to the play itself. At the point in ancient history in which *Julius Caesar* is set, Rome was becoming slightly more democratic—well, democratic in their terms, not in modern ones. Tribunes, meant as representatives of the people, were being elected in order to protect them from the rigors of tyranny. Thus, to have a man like Caesar, charismatic and fresh from military triumph, come into the city and begin to establish himself as a supreme ruler was a dangerous trend. It is not surprising, then, that Flavius and Marullus behave as they do at the beginning of the play. They are, in effect, doing their job properly and to an Elizabethan audience their behavior, despite its autocratic tone to a modern reader's ears, would have been perfectly acceptable and should have been met with obedience and respect. The carpenter and cobbler, however, are barely under control and show little respect, although they do ultimately obey.

But it is not the masses who are the problem in this play. The real failure is that the ruling class does not rule properly. Instead of uniting for the good of the people as they ought to, they imagine themselves as individuals forming small splinter groups that, in the end undermine genuine authority. By disabling themselves in this way, the aristocratic class can still manipulate unruly plebeians but cannot keep them in check.

As a member of that class, Brutus is as much at fault as anyone else. It is, in fact, tempting to think of Brutus as an entirely sympathetic character. At the end of the play, the audience hears extravagant words of praise: "This was the noblest Roman of them all" and "This was a man." By this point, however, readers ought to mistrust their reactions to such praise. Antony and Octavius have shown themselves to be perfectly capable of using and misusing language in order to establish their own positions, and the play has given ample evidence of a tendency to objectify the dead rather than to remember them as they actually were.

To be fair, there are gradations of character fault in this play and Brutus is more sympathetic than other characters. He does indeed believe that what he has done by murdering Caesar was necessary, and believes that anyone who hears his rationale will side with him. His very naïveté suggests innocence. On the other hand, upon examining his soliloquy in Act II, Scene 1, note that Brutus must do a fair amount to convince himself that Caesar must die: He has to admit that Caesar has not yet done anything wrong and so decides that his violent act will be preemptory, heading off the inevitable results of Caesar's ambition. Brutus' dilemma is that he has bought into the belief that if one lives life entirely by a philosophy—in his case one of logic and reason — everyone will be all right. He denies any other viewpoint and so is as blinded as Caesar is deaf. Before praising Brutus as Antony does after his death, remember that Brutus brought himself and the state of Rome to a point of such instability.

Antony, another member of that ruling class, is also one of the more sympathetic characters of the play. But is he a good ruler? The audience may like him for his emotion. His outrage at the murder of Caesar and his tears over Caesar's corpse are undoubtedly genuine. His revenge is partly fuelled by the horror and anger he feels at the outrage, and the reader is drawn to such loyalty. In addition, the skill that he exhibits in his manipulation of theatrical effects and language during his funeral oration is powerful and attractive. Yet, Antony is culpable too. While his emotional response is undoubtedly justified, it, too, contributes to unrest and political instability. While he, Octavius, and Lepidus ultimately form a triumvirate to return the state to stability, in fact, that it is a ruling structure fraught with problems. Lepidus is weak and a power struggle is on the horizon for Antony and Octavius. (In Shakespeare's *Antony and Cleopatra*, Octavius is the ultimate winner of that struggle.)

A World Without Women

"This was a man" is Antony's final tribute to Brutus. Brutus' reputation, damaged as it has been by his participation in the conspiracy, and by his rather self-deluding rationale for it, has been reclaimed. It has been reclaimed partially because his character, defined at the beginning of the play as entirely masculine, has taken on some feminine characteristics, such as grief over his wife's death, love for his friend, and tender concern for his followers. By the end of the play, Brutus' character is more fully-rounded but is the world he leaves us better off? Can it be when the world left behind is entirely without women? Shakespeare takes the opportunity in *Julius Caesar* to say both "yes" and "no." At times, characters take on so-called feminine characteristics and lose their ability to rule well. At other times, characters like Brutus gain a great deal from incorporating the feminine into their own personalities. Shakespeare's suggestion is that while a balance can be struck and an ideal attained, it is ultimately unworkable.

You find only two female characters in Julius Caesar. The first, Calphurnia, is Caesar's wife, and is emblematic of one standard sexist Elizabethan understanding of woman. She is a shrew. She controls instead of being controlled. She exists as a foil for her husband's character. By her strength, the audience sees what Caesar ought to be; by her conscience, what his ought to be; by her death, what he ought to be prepared to do. For this reason, her character is not developed on a psychological level in the way that Caesar's is.

The reader's first contact with her is during the feast of Lupercal. Caesar asks Antony to touch her as he passes her in the race that is a part of the celebrations. Caesar asks this because Calphurnia is childless, and superstition dictates that the touch of the athlete during this holy feast will make her fertile. The implication, then, is that she is at fault for not producing an heir. In fact, the implication is that Caesar is no longer potent enough to impregnate her. His request of the athletic womanizer, Antony, is an indication of Caesar's own effeminacy.

Such is the root of Caesar's downfall. He has taken on too many feminine characteristics. His prowess is in the past and is only momentarily evident in Act II, Scene 2 when he refuses to listen to Calphurnia's worries about what will happen if he goes to the Capitol. "Caesar shall forth. The things that threatened me / Ne'er looked but on my back; when they shall see / The face of Caesar, they are vanished." However, he is convinced, bowing to her hysteria and his mind is changed only after Decius embarrasses him. "[I]t were a mock / Apt to be rendered for someone to say / 'Break up the Senate till another time, / When Caesar's wife shall meet with better dreams.'" On to his own death.

Portia is a much more interesting character on her own and yet she, too, is really only portrayed through her relationship with men. Her relationship with her husband is clearly one of intimacy and respect. She speaks openly with him about the unrest he has recently exhibited and forces him to speak to her and tell her what is going on.

Note, however, how she does this. Brutus does not want her to know what is going on. She changes his mind by pressing him to define her in one of the two ways in which a woman can be defined in this society: She is either a good Roman woman worthy of his secrets, well-wived and well-fathered, or she is "Brutus' harlot." Faced with this distinction, Brutus can only choose to tell her what is happening. Unfortunately for Portia, the knowledge that he imparts is her downfall. In Act II, Scene 4 Portia complains that she has "a man's mind, but a woman's might." She has been given access to a man's knowledge but because of her position as a woman, she is unable to use it and must sit and wait for the outcome of men's affairs. Such knowledge is too much for her and she commits suicide in the very garden in which she first heard Brutus' secrets.

With this, Portia is gone from the play, and the reader never again sees a female character. What the audience does see, however, is a transference of Portia's feminine qualities to her husband by means of his relationship with Cassius. At the beginning of the play, the relationship between these two men was less than profound. They are connected by a common desire to overturn Caesar's tyranny but have entirely different motivations. In addition, Cassius' approach toward convincing Brutus to join him has been cynical to say the least.

By Act IV, Scene 2, their relationship has become a friendship, and it has become a friendship that has the decided qualities of a love relationship. In Act IV, Scene 2, Brutus has taken offense at what he believes was Cassius' refusal to send money when he needed it. Cassius is quite taken aback by this accusation and the conversation quickly descends into a "yes you did, no I didn't" affair that almost results in a fight. Cassius is innocent of the offense and is hurt that he is "Hated by one he loves, braved by his brother."

What motivates Brutus to this anger? It turns out that it is grief over Portia's death. It is to Cassius that Brutus turns in his grief. The grief that he feels, the loss, the sense of betrayal are all translated into anger toward this friend, and after those emotions are spent, the two men are closer in some ways than Brutus ever was with Portia. The latter relationship shares the same respect for each other and the same sharing of intimacy, yet it is a relationship that can operate in the same spheres because it encompasses a level of equality not possible between a woman and a man.

From that moment, the audience has an increasing amount of sympathy for Brutus, who has been humanized by his wife's death. While he clearly loved his wife, there was also some distance between them, partly because of her rather stoic nature (remember her self-wounding), partly because he is unwilling to confide in her. This combination of the masculine and the feminine in her character was not a completely appropriate one. It was unworkable given the way in which the Roman world worked. The flip side, of course, was Caesar's behavior. His combination of femininity and masculinity was also unworkable. With their deaths, Brutus is able to incorporate both aspects of their personalities, most directly from his wife, given her more moral nature. With the banishment of women and inappropriate femininity from Rome, the state ought to be a better one. But there is an unattractive sterility to such a world. What has been created is an unworkable ideal. Brutus' death is an indication of just how unworkable it is.

Theater within a Theater within a Theater

How many ages hence
Shall this our lofty scene be acted over,
In states unborn and accents yet unknown!

Cassius speaks these words in Act 3, Scene 1 just as he convinces the exultant conspirators to smear their hands with Caesar's blood. At this moment of highest drama, one of the chief actors of this piece draws attention to its theatricality. Why?

It is a common trope of Elizabethan thinking to draw attention to life's fictions. Queen Elizabeth staged many public processions and scenes and created and lived the role of the Virgin Queen. Her subjects were both her fellow actors and her audience. Playwrights of the time, and Shakespeare in particular, made use of this metaphor in a number of ways (for an interesting example, take a look at *Hamlet* and the play within a play, *The Mousetrap*).

In *Julius Caesar*, theatricality is both an example of one of the major themes of the play, persuasion, and a comment on the deterioration of the state of Rome. A number of characters use theater in an attempt to persuade.

During the first meeting of Cassius and Brutus, (Act I, Scene 2), they hear a number of shouts. Later in the scene, Casca enters and reports on the offstage theater that has taken place. Caesar has staged a mock refusal of the crown, thinking that he will build a desire in his audience (the plebeians) that he eventually accept it. Think of this as someone refusing an award, saying, "Oh no, I couldn't possibly . . . oh no . . . well, if you insist." (For another example of this dramatic effect, one which works more successfully for the protagonist, see Shakespeare's *Richard III.*) Caesar's stage managing backfires though, and instead of acclaiming him, the people behave like a real audience passing judgement on the quality of the spectacle. "If the tag-rag people did not clap him and hiss him / according as he pleased and displeased them, as they use to / do the players in the theatre." Caesar's performance isn't good enough. It proves his superficiality. The people perceive this and refuse to accept him as their ruler.

Antony is much more successful with his theatrics. Unfortunately, Brutus does not recognize what Antony is up to when he asks to give Caesar's funeral oration in Act III, Scene 2. The opportunity to stage a scene is evident to the reader and to at least one of the conspirators, Cassius, who tries to dissuade Brutus, but to no avail. Imagine the power of Antony's entrance as he bears Caesar's body in his arms. This is an exhibition meant to move an audience—and it works. Antony's persuasive rhetoric that follows allows him to realize his objective: to incite the mob to revolt against the conspirators, with another showy scene.

When Antony gradually uncovers Caesar's body and exposes its wounds, the first Plebeian responds with "O piteous spectacle" and that is precisely what it is. By means of the theatrical, then, the people have been convinced to act, not in their own best interests but in the interests of Antony, Octavius, and Lepidus. Theater's power has been to continue the strife rather than to resolve it. To an Elizabethan audience, such dramatic tension would have been both threatening and seductive.

CliffsNotes Review

Use this CliffsNotes Review to test your understanding of the original text, and reinforce what you've learned in this book. After you work through the essay questions and useful practice projects, you're well on your way to understanding a comprehensive and meaningful interpretation of *Julius Caesar*.

Essay Questions

1. Describe the changes that occur in the friendship between Cassius and Brutus.

2. The characters in this play are very concerned with what it was and is to be Roman. What role does tradition play in *Julius Caesar*?

3. Does Caesar have any real impact on the action of the play? Before his death? After his death?

4. What role does the supernatural play?

Practice Projects

1. Create your own Web site. Consider what you may put on such a site. Do you want to take a general approach and include a summary of the play with your own commentaries and character sketches? Or do you want to create a niche Web site dedicated to specific information, such as reviews of *Julius Caesar* on film? Remember to include appropriate graphics and links to other sites you find useful.

2. Write another play with a different setting, cast of characters, and/or outcome. What if, for example, Portia got together with Calphurnia and stopped the conspiracy? What if the actors in this play went home and found violence, conspiracy, betrayal, and great friendship in their own lives? Take the original as your inspiration, but use your imagination. The sky's the limit.

3. Research productions of *Julius Caesar* over the centuries, in other countries or in your hometown. What did they include from the original, what did they cut, and what did they change? Why? Stage your own production making your own choices or write an essay describing the most interesting of these productions.

4. Julius Caesar, Brutus, and Mark Antony were all real people. Do some research on who they were. Look at Shakespeare's source, Plutarch's *Lives*, as well as modern histories. Write an essay on historical objectivity. Is such objectivity possible? What role does art have in forming our ideas of the past?

CliffsNotes Resource Center

The learning doesn't need to stop here. CliffsNotes Resource Center shows you the best of the best—links to the best information in print and online about the author and/or related works. And don't think that this is all we've prepared for you; we've put all kinds of pertinent information at www.cliffsnotes.com. Look for all the terrific resources at your favorite bookstore or local library and on the Internet. When you're online, make your first stop www.cliffsnotes.com where you'll find more incredibly useful information about *Julius Caesar*.

Books and Articles

This CliffsNotes book, published by Wiley Publishing, Inc., provides a meaningful interpretation of *Julius Caesar*. If you are looking for information about the author and/or related works, check out these other publications:

BLOOM, HAROLD, Ed. William Shakespeare's "Julius Caesar." New York: Chelsea House, 1988. A collection of nine critical essays *Julius Caesar,* arranged in order of their original publication.

MILES, GARY B. "How Roman are Shakespeare's 'Romans'?" *Shakespeare Quarterly* 40 (1989): 257–83.

MIOLA, ROBERT S. "Julius Caesar and the Tyrannicide Debate." *Renaissance Quarterly* 38 (1985): 271–89.

PASTER, GAIL. "'In the Spirit of Men There Is No Blood': Blood as a Trope of Gender in Julius Caesar." *Renaissance Quarterly* 40 (1989): 284–98.

It's easy to find books published by Wiley Publishing, Inc. and other publishers. You'll find them in your favorite bookstores (on the Internet and at a store near you). We also have three Web sites that you can use to read about all the books we publish:

- www.cliffsnotes.com

- www.dummies.com

- www.wiley.com

Internet

Check out these Web resources for more information about William Shakespeare and *Julius Caesar*.

Perseus Project, www.perseus.tufts.edu/JC/—is an ever-expanding site dedicated to Shakespeare's *Julius Caesar*. The site offers information on Shakespeare's text, sources, and analogues, and posts student projects.

Shakespeare's Life and Times, Web.uvic.ca/shakespeare/Library/SLT/fset_whole.htm?page=introsubj,book=intro—offers information on Shakespeare's life and times, including important historical, philosophical, cultural, and theatrical context. This site also offers links to discussions of *Julius Caesar*, as well as other of Shakespeare's plays.

Shakespeare in Europe, www.unibas.ch/shine/SHINE_Links.htm—is a well-maintained, comprehensive page of links on Shakespeare and related subjects. You'll find everything from scholarly comment to libraries and other resources to Just for Fun. Look for sections on Shakespeare and Film and Shakespeare in the Classroom.

The Internet Movie Database and Library of Congress movie and TV resources, www.us.imdb.com and gopher://marvel.loc.gov:70/00/research/reading.rooms/motion.picture/mopic.tv/mpfind/willfilm—allows you to search for English and foreign films and TV productions.

Next time you're on the Internet, don't forget to drop by www.cliffsnotes.com. We've created an online Resource Center that you can use today, tomorrow, and beyond.

Send Us Your Favorite Tips

In your quest for knowledge, have you ever experienced that sublime moment when you figure out a trick that saves time or trouble? Perhaps you realized you were taking ten steps to accomplish something that could have taken two. Or you found a little-known workaround that achieved great results. If you've discovered a useful tup that helped you understand Julius Caesar more effectively and you'd like to share it, the CliffsNotes staff would love to hear from you. Go to our Web site at www.cliffs-notes.com and click the Talk to Us button. If we select your tip, we may publish it as part of CliffsNotes Daily, our exciting, free e-mail newsletter. To find out more or to subscribe to a newsletter, go to www.cliffsnotes.com on the Web.

Index

A

Antony, 10, 11, 30, 43, 44
    character analysis, 80, 81, 82
    character faults, 91
    conspirators' regard of, 32
    derision of Brutus at Philippi, 65
    emotional nature of, 56
    eulogy for Brutus, 10, 75, 92
    funeral oration, 9, 43, 49, 50, 51, 95
    in footrace, 21, 22
    influence on Caesar, 23
    perception of loyalty, 73
    plan for vengeance, 45
    power struggle with Octavius, 55, 65, 66
    questionable honesty of, 8
    reputation of, 11
    request to be resolved with
      conspirators, 43
    revocation of Caesar's will, 55
    social nature of, 38
Antony and Cleopatra, 5
Artemidorus, 43
    note to Caesar, 40
    opinion of Caesar, 40
Athena, 33
augurers, 37

B

Blackfriars Theatre, 4
blood imagery, 32
broken-back plays, 4
Brutus
    address of crowd, 49, 50
    appearance of Caesar's ghost, 10, 11,
      61, 62
    as hero, 76
    as leader of conspirators, 31
    battle strategy, 60, 69
    character analysis, 84, 85, 86
    character faults, 91
    conversion of, 26
    death of, 10, 75, 76
    echo of soothsayer's warning, 22
    farewell to dead Cassius, 70

    feminine characteristics of, 8, 92
    flight from Rome, 49
    friendship with Cassius, 58, 71, 93
    letters to, 24, 30, 31
    motivations of, 71
    musings on battle, 66
    noblilty of, 11
    opposition to Caesar, 8
    opposition to killing Antony, 32
    parting with Cassius at Philippi, 65
    persuasion by Cassius, 21, 22
    quarrel with Cassius, 58, 60, 61
    reaction to Portia's death, 61, 94
    reclamation of reputation, 92
    renewal of friendship with Cassius, 60
    self-delusion of, 31, 91
    soliloquy on Caesar's character, 30
    speech to crowd, 9
    sympathy with conspirators, 7, 9, 24
    transfer of love for Portia, 61

C

Caesar, 11
    character analysis, 79, 80
    conspiracy against, 9. See also
      conspirators
    crowning of, 7
    deafness of, 27
    decision to go to Senate, 37
    decorated statues of, 19
    effeminacy of, 8, 38, 92
    ghost of, 10, 11, 61, 62
    impotence of, 22, 92
    masculinity of, 38
    murder of, 9, 43, 44
    overthrow of ruling class, 19
    past greatness of, 40
    persuasion by Calphurnia, 37
    procession to Capitol, 9, 39
    public celebration for, 18
    refusal of crown, 21, 23, 95
    soothsayer's warning, 8, 22
    suspicion of Cassius, 21, 23
    triumphant return of, 8, 21
    weaknesses of, 22, 23, 27, 38
    will of, 55
Caius Ligarius, 31
Calphurnia
    as foil to Caesar, 92
    barrenness of, 21, 22
    characterization of, 38, 92
    nightmares of, 9, 37

NOTES

NOTES